# OKLAHOMA'S 100 GREATEST ATHLETES

## BERRY TRAMEL and BOB BURKE
### Foreword by BARRY SWITZER

Series Editor: Gini Moore Campbell
Associate Editors: Eric Dabney and Natalie Taylor

Printed in Canada.

ISBN 978-1-938923-15-9

Library of Congress Catalog Number 2015934238

Designed by Nathan Dunn

UNLESS OTHERWISE NOTED, PHOTOGRAPHS COURTESY
OKLAHOMA PUBLISHING COMPANY

# Oklahoma Heritage Association

# ACKNOWLEDGMENTS

The authors are grateful for the assistance of our editors, Gini Moore Campbell, Eric Dabney, and Natalie Taylor; and for photographs and editorial assistance from Justin Lenhart at the Jim Thorpe Association and Oklahoma Sports Hall of Fame; Linda Lynn at the Oklahoma Publishing Company; Doug Self at Southwestern Oklahoma State University; Mike Houck and Renata Hays at the University of Oklahoma; Ron Shelton; and Murray Evans at Oklahoma Christian University.

# CONTENTS

Foreword vii
Introduction xi
Jim Thorpe 1
Mickey Mantle 2
Barry Sanders 3
John Smith 4
Shannon Miller 5
Lee Roy Selmon 6
Kevin Durant 7
Carl Hubbell 8
Steve Largent 9
Johnny Bench 10
Adrian Peterson 11
Troy Aikman 12
Jess Willard 13
Bob Kurland 14
Don McNeill 15
Will Shields 16
Wilbur "Bullet Joe" Rogan 17
Tommy McDonald 18
Paul Waner 19
Mark Price 20
Jim Shoulders 21
Nancy Lopez 22
Marques Haynes 23
Thurman Thomas 24
Yojiro Uetake 25
Allie Reynolds 26
Russell Westbrook 27
Sean O'Grady 28
Susan Maxwell Berning 29
Alvan Adams 30
Wayman Tisdale 31
Mark Schultz 32
Billy Sims 33
Kenny Monday 34
Blake Griffin 35
Spec Sanders 36
Crystal Robinson 37
Charles Coe 38

Hubert "Geese" Ausbie 39
Carl Mays 40
Doll Harris 41
Chris Paul 42
Ace Gutowsky 43
Ida Davenport 44
Mat Hoffman 45
Bobby Boyd 46
Jack McCracken 47
Roy Williams 48
Lloyd Waner 49
Dennis Rodman 50
Clendon Thomas 51
Danny Hodge 52
Leslie O'Neal 53
Greg Pruitt 54
Joe Dial 55
Joe Washington 56
Dave Schultz 57
Jon Kolb 58
Bobby Murcer 59
Easy Jet 60
Joe Carter 61
Jim Barnes 62
Pepper Martin 63
Ralph Neely 64
Michele Smith 65
Kendall Cross 66
Mookie Blaylock 67
Keith Johnson 68
Stacey Dales 69
Walt Garrison 70
Steve Owens 71
Roy Duvall 72
Bart Conner 73
Jerry Sherk 74
Johny Hendricks 75
Gil Morgan 76
Arnold Short 77
Don Butler 78

Glenn Dobbs 79
Lindy McDaniel 80
Scott Verplank 81
Bryant Reeves 82
Bobby Ussery 83
Sam Bradford 84
Drew Pearson 85
Kelly Garrison 86
Jerry Tubbs 87
Matt Kemp 88
Billy Caskey 89
John Starks 90
Tony Casillas 91
Jeff Bennett 92
Tom Churchill 93
Wes Welker 94
Cindy Yan Fang 95
Jerry Shipp 96
Gerald McCoy 97
Robin Ventura 98
Serge Ibake 99
Virgil Franklin 100
Honorable Mention 101
FCA Turns 60 105
The Birth of the Oklahoma
Sports Hall of Fame 106
Members of the Oklahoma
Sports Hall of Fame 108

# FOREWORD

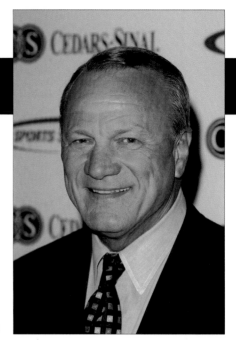

## BY COACH BARRY SWITZER

Oklahomans have always excelled in sports competition. The high level of achievement began with Jim Thorpe's domination of the world sports stage at the 1912 Olympic Games. He was called "the greatest athlete in the world." The excellence continued as Oklahoma athletes began "giving it their best effort" in high school and college competition in the young state.

It was not long after statehood that Oklahoma began producing national stars in baseball, football, and basketball. Many local boys made the big leagues in baseball and amateur and college basketball teams took national titles in the 1930s and 1940s. Oklahoma A & M was the first college in the nation to win back-to-back NCAA basketball championships.

After World War II, football became the favorite sport of many supporters of Oklahoma high school and college programs. The University of Oklahoma became the number one sports venue as the Sooners played football weekly before the largest gathering of fans in the history of the state.

However, Oklahoma athletes' success in the last half of the twentieth century has not been limited to football, baseball, and basketball. Oklahomans have won world and Olympic championships in wrestling, gymnastics, softball, and rodeo.

In any sport, wherever played and at whatever level of competition, Oklahoma athletes rise to the top. Oklahoma is truly the home of champions!

# INTRODUCTION

It is a highly subjective and difficult task to pick the best 100 athletes from the thousands of Oklahoma men and women who have excelled in collegiate and professional sports competition. To make the task tolerable, we have established strict criteria.

**HOW TO MAKE THE LIST**—We put great stock in an athlete spending his or her formative years in Oklahoma, learning the sport that made them famous. Being born in Oklahoma is not enough to make our list, especially if the athlete moved from the Sooner State at an early age and learned to play his or her sport elsewhere. A great example is Willie Stargell, a member of the National Baseball Hall of Fame, who was born in Earlsboro, Oklahoma. However, Stargell's family moved to California when he was two years old and his connection with Oklahoma was never re-established. Hall of Famer Dizzy Dean lived for a short time in eastern Oklahoma, but his Oklahoma connection was never strong.

We also have excluded from the list the great Warren Spahn, the winningest left-handed pitcher in major league baseball history. Spahn was born and raised in New York. During World War II he was assigned to Camp Gruber near Muskogee. He soon made Oklahoma his home for the rest of his life. Baseball Hall of Famer Ferguson Jenkins lived in Oklahoma for many years after his retirement. Based upon our criteria, Jenkins also is not included in our list.

The same goes for Joe "Iron Man" McGinnity, who lived out his life in McAlester. He was one of major league baseball's all-time strongmen of the late 1890s and early 1900s. He still holds the record for most complete games in a season.

**HOW WE RANKED THEM**—Athletes were judged on their achievements at the highest possible level of completion of their particular sport. For that reason, Kelli Litsch, considered by many to be one of the greatest women's college basketball players ever, did not choose to play professionally, and is listed only in Honorable Mention. Heisman Trophy winners Billy Vessels and Jason White did not make the list, and other Heisman winners Steve Owens and Billy Sims, although incredible college players, rank much lower on the list than less-decorated college stars who had outstanding professional careers.

Berry Tramel and Bob Burke, 2015

## JIM THORPE 1
### POTTAWATOMIE COUNTY

There is really no serious debate as to who is Oklahoma's greatest athlete. In fact, Jim Thorpe may be the most versatile athlete in American history. Born of Sac and Fox Indian blood near Prague, Indian Territory, in 1888, Thorpe played college football at Carlisle Indian School and starred in professional football. He won gold medals in the decathlon and pentathlon at the 1912 Olympics. He also played major league baseball.

Thorpe was the first president of what became the National Football League. His statue stands at the entrance of the Pro Football Hall of Fame in Canton, Ohio. The Associated Press (AP) named Thorpe the greatest athlete of the first half of the twentieth century. At the end of the century, AP listed him the third greatest athlete of the entire century behind Babe Ruth and Michael Jordan. Thorpe died in 1953 at age 64.

*Courtesy Oklahoma State Senate Historical Preservation Fund, Inc.*

# MICKEY MANTLE
## COMMERCE

**2**

Born in 1931 in Spavinaw, and raised in nearby Commerce, Mantle is second only to Babe Ruth in universal popularity among many baseball fans. He played his entire 18-year major league career for the New York Yankees. He was a starter in 16 All Star games and was American League Most Valuable Player three times.

*Courtesy National Baseball Hall of Fame.*

Mantle played on seven world championship clubs and still holds several World Series records, including most career home runs and runs batted in. The Yankees retired his famous number "7". In 1956, Mantle was as good a baseball player as God ever made. A lightning fast, 24-year-old centerfielder who hit 52 home runs, scored 132 runs, and drove in 130, playing in a pitcher's park. Mantle won the American League home run title by 20 dingers.

A member of the National Baseball Hall of Fame, Mantle died at age 63 in 1995. In 2015, more than 40 years after Mantle's retirement from baseball, there were more than 4,000 Mantle memorabilia items on eBay, far more than any other baseball star.

*Courtesy Pro Football Hall of Fame.*

## BARRY SANDERS
### OKLAHOMA STATE UNIVERSITY

**3**

Born in Wichita, Kansas, Sanders did not play running back until the fourth game of his senior year in high school. Not highly recruited because of his 5'8" size, he picked Oklahoma State University to play college football. For his first two years at OSU, he backed up Thurman Thomas. In his junior year, 1988, Sanders led the nation in rushing and scoring and set 34 NCAA records. For his banner year, he was awarded the Heisman Trophy. In 2008, ESPN named him the second best college football player of all time.

Drafted by the Detroit Lions, Sanders had a brilliant NFL career. In ten seasons, he rushed for more than 15,000 yards and was within one season of eclipsing Walter Payton's career rushing mark. Sanders was the first NFL player to rush for more than 1,000 yards in ten consecutive seasons. The notion that Sanders played on bad Detroit Lions teams is false. The Lions were 78-82 in the regular season during Sanders' career but made the playoffs in five of Sanders' 10 seasons. In 2004, he was inducted into the Pro Football Hall of Fame.

# JOHN SMITH
## DEL CITY & OKLAHOMA STATE UNIVERSITY

4

Smith was a champion wrestler at Del City High School before beginning a stunning collegiate career at OSU where he won 154 bouts with only seven losses, the best won-loss record of any Cowboy wrestler.

*Courtesy Oklahoma Hall of Fame.*

His domestic freestyle record is 80-0 and his international freestyle record is 100-5.

Smith was the first wrestler to win the Sullivan Award as the nation's outstanding amateur athlete. At OSU, he won back-to-back NCAA championships in 1987 and 1988. In addition, he won four world wrestling championships and two Olympic gold medals. In 1988, he was named Man of the Year by *Amateur Wrestling News*. He was acclaimed as the world's best amateur wrestler in 1991 by the Federation International de Lutte Amateur, the international governing body for amateur wrestling.

Smith was inducted into the National Wrestling Hall of Fame in 1997. Many experts consider him to be the greatest American wrestler ever.

In 1993, Smith became wrestling coach at OSU where he has won five NCAA national championships.

# SHANNON MILLER
## EDMOND

# 5

Miller is the most decorated gymnast in American history. She was raised in Edmond after her family moved from her native Missouri. In high school she won the Dial Award in 1994, the most coveted high school sports award. She won a combined 16 World Championships and Olympic medals between 1991 and 1996. She was the most successful American athlete, by medal count—two silvers and three bronzes—at the Barcelona Olympics in 1992. In 1996, in Atlanta, Georgia, she won two Olympic gold medals.

Miller is the only American amateur athlete to win the Sullivan Award three times—1993, 1994, and 1995.

## LEE ROY SELMON
### EUFAULA & UNIVERSITY OF OKLAHOMA

6

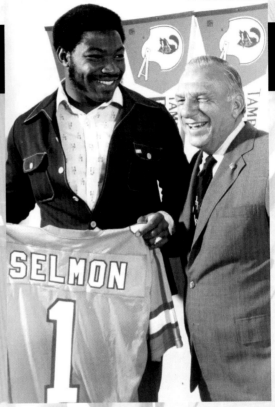

*Courtesy Oklahoma Hall of Fame.*

Born in Eufaula, the youngest of nine children, Lee Roy is a member of the College Football and Pro Football Hall of Fame. In 1973, he joined brothers Lucious and Dewey on the OU defensive line. He became a bonafide star in 1974, anchoring one of OU's best defenses. The Sooners won the national championship in 1974 and 1975 as Lee Roy won the Lombardi Award and the Outland Trophy in the latter year. Coach Barry Switzer called him the best player he ever coached. Known as "The Gentle Giant," Lee Roy was later named to the *Sports Illustrated* college football All-Century team.

A consensus All American, he was the top NFL draft choice in 1976, picked by Tampa Bay where he played his entire nine-year pro football career. He was selected for the Pro Bowl six times, a member of the NFL 1980s All Decade Team, the 1979 NFL Defensive Lineman of the Year, and co-MVP of the 1982 Pro Bowl. When Lee Roy retired, the Buccaneers retired his # 63. He died in 2011.

## KEVIN DURANT 7
### OKLAHOMA CITY THUNDER

A native of Washington, D.C., Durant played college basketball at the University of Texas where he was an All-American and consensus National Player of the Year. He was selected second overall in the 2007 NBA draft by the Seattle SuperSonics, a year before the franchise moved to Oklahoma City. He was NBA Rookie of the Year in 2008. In 2014, he was the Most Valuable Player of the NBA and won the scoring title for the fourth time in the past five years.

Durant's charm and willingness to help worthy causes have elevated him to hero status in the community. Since arriving in Oklahoma, he has become one of the most recognizable names and faces in world sports. His jersey sales are near the top around the globe and he frequently appears in national commercials.

# CARL HUBBELL
## MEEKER

8

Hubbell, elected to the National Baseball Hall of Fame in 1947, was one of major league baseball's most effective pitchers from 1928 to 1943. Born in Missouri, but raised in Meeker, he spent his entire 16-year career with the New York Giants. With a masterful screwball,

*Courtesy National Baseball Hall of Fame.*

Hubbell set the major league record for 24 consecutive victories in 1936 and 1937 and won 253 games in his career. He was an All Star nine times.

In the 1934 All Star game, he struck out five future Hall-of-Famers in a row—Babe Ruth, Lou Gehrig, Jimmie Foxx, Al Simmons, and Joe Cronin. On another occasion he pitched an 18-inning shutout without walking a single batter. Hubbell was the first player in the National League to have his number retired. Until his death in an automobile accident in 1988, he was director of player development and a scout for the Giants for 45 years.

## STEVE LARGENT
### PUTNAM CITY & UNIVERSITY OF TULSA
**9**

*Courtesy Pro Football Hall of Fame.*

Born in Tulsa, Largent was the starting catcher on the Putnam City High School baseball team that included future major league pitcher Bob Shirley and NFL quarterback Pat Ryan. Largent chose football for college and the University of Tulsa. He led the nation in touchdown catches in 1974 and 1975 and was All American in 1975.

Largent was not taken until the fourth round of the NFL draft by the Houston Oilers and was promptly traded to Seattle for an eighth-round draft choice. Fourteen seasons later, Largent retired from the NFL holding six career records, including receptions, touchdown catches, total yards by a receiver, and 1,000-yard seasons.

Known for his community and civic involvement, Largent was the NFL Walter Payton Man of the Year in 1988. From 1994 to 2002, he was a member of Congress from Oklahoma. He was elected to the Pro Football Hall of Fame in 1995. Largent was the Republican nominee for governor of Oklahoma in 2002.

# JOHNNY BENCH
## BINGER

**10**

*Courtesy National Baseball Hall of Fame.*

Bench, elected to the National Baseball Hall of Fame in 1989 during his first year of eligibility, was born in Oklahoma City but raised in Binger where he played baseball and basketball and was the class valedictorian.

During 17 years with the Cincinnati Reds, Bench became one of the greatest catchers in baseball history. During his career, the Reds won two World Series, four pennants, and six division titles. Bench was National League Rookie of the Year, won the Gold Glove ten consecutive years, and was named to the National League All Star team 13 years in a row from 1968 to 1980. He was National League MVP in 1970 and 1972 and MVP of the 1976 World Series with a .533 average.

Bench was elected to the Hall of Fame with the third-highest total in history. He was named on 96 percent of ballots cast by baseball writers around the country.

# ADRIAN PETERSON
## UNIVERSITY OF OKLAHOMA

**11**

A native of Palestine, Texas, Peterson was an All-American running back at OU. He set the NCAA freshman rushing record in 2004 and was the first freshman to finish as runner-up in the Heisman Trophy balloting and the first freshman at OU to be recognized as a First-Team Associated Press All-American. He was the first round pick of the Minnesota Vikings in the 2007 NFL draft and immediately launched a stellar professional career.

In his first NFL season, Peterson was Offensive Rookie of the Year and set the rookie rushing record. He also set a new NFL record for most yards rushing in a single game (296). He is second all-time in rushing yards in a season, has the most 50-plus yard runs in a season, and was NFL Most Valuable Player in 2012. In 2013, he became the third fastest player to reach 10,000 rushing yards in NFL history.

# TROY AIKMAN
## HENRYETTA

**12**

Aikman was born in California but his family moved to a farm near Henryetta when he was 12. He was an All State high school baseball and football star. He began his college football career at OU, but broke his ankle in his first year as a starter. Coach Barry Switzer oversaw Aikman's transfer to UCLA where he won the Davey O'Brien Award as the nation's top quarterback in 1988. A consensus All American, he finished third in the 1988 Heisman Trophy voting.

*Courtesy Pro Football Hall of Fame.*

The top draft choice of the Dallas Cowboys in 1989, Aikman became one of pro football's greatest quarterbacks. From 1989 to 2000, he was selected for six Pro Bowls while the Cowboys won three Super Bowl championships. He was MVP of Super Bowl XXVII. He is a member of the College and Pro Football Halls of Fame. Since his retirement he has worked for Fox Sports as an NFL television analyst.

## JESS WILLARD
### ELK CITY

**13**

Willard was born in Kansas but drifted south to Elk City shortly after 1900 to work as a cowboy. He was nearly 30 when he began learning to box at the Oklahoma City Athletic Club. His first eight boxing matches were in Oklahoma.

In 1915, in Havana, Cuba, Willard knocked out champion Jack Johnson to win the world heavyweight boxing championship. Willard was 6'7" and weighed 245 pounds, the largest heavyweight champion until Primo Carnera won the title in 1933.

At age 37, Willard lost his crown to Jack Dempsey on July 4, 1919, in Toledo, Ohio. He was 35-6 in his heavyweight career, with 20 wins by knockout. He died in 1968.

Kurland is the only three-time All American to play basketball at Oklahoma State University. He was the first big man in college basketball and the first to regularly dunk the ball during games. In fact, the NCAA banned goaltending in 1945 largely because Kurland jumped above the rim to block opponents' shots.

Born in Missouri, Kurland helped Coach Henry Iba and OSU win back-to-back NCAA men's basketball championships in 1945 and 1946. In his four seasons at OSU, Kurland established records for career points and free throw attempts that still stand.

Kurland passed up the infant NBA in 1946 and opted to play with the AAU Phillips 66ers of the National Industrial Basketball League. He played on the best amateur team of the era. The 66ers were 52-2 in 1946-1947 and 62-3 in the 1947-1948 campaign. Kurland played six seasons for the 66ers, winning the national AAU championship three times.

As an amateur, he was eligible for the Olympics and played on the gold medal United States squads in 1952 and 1956. He was inducted into the National Basketball Hall of Fame in 1961.

## DON McNEILL
### OKLAHOMA CITY

# 15

Easily Oklahoma's greatest tennis player ever, McNeill won five state tennis titles and claimed numerous national championships. He was ranked in the top ten players in the world six years between 1937 and 1946.

McNeill was born in Chickasha but graduated from Classen High School in Oklahoma City after learning to play tennis as a ball boy at the Oklahoma City Tennis Club. He wanted to go to OU or Texas, but neither invited him. Instead, he went to college at Kenyon College in Ohio.

In 1939, he beat tournament favorite Bobby Riggs in the French Open, only the second American to win the title. He won three of America's most prestigious tennis titles, the National Clay Court, the National Intercollegiate, and the U.S. Nationals. He was the top collegiate player, the national champion, and the number one ranked player in the nation in 1939.

World War II took several years of McNeill's prime. He was a Navy intelligence officer but managed to win four consecutive championships in Argentina while stationed there. He was inducted into the International Tennis Hall of Fame in 1965. He died in 1996.

# WILL SHIELDS
## LAWTON

**16**

Shields was born in Kansas but grew up in Lawton where he was a high school football star. Recruited by the University of Nebraska, Shields played for the Cornhuskers from 1989 to 1992. He was a consensus All American and Outland Trophy winner in his final year at Nebraska.

In 1999, he was selected as a member of the Nebraska All-Century Football Team in a fan poll. He also was selected as an offensive guard by the Walter Camp Foundation on its All-Century team.

Shields played his entire 14-year NFL career for the Kansas City Chiefs. He was selected to the Pro Bowl 12 times and won the Walter Payton NFL Man of the Year Award in 2003. He retired at the end of the 2006 season. In his pro career, Shields never missed a game, and he failed to start in only one contest, his first regular-season game as a rookie in 1993. He owns a sports facility and gymnasium in a Kansas City suburb. In 2015, Shields was inducted into the Pro Football Hall of Fame.

# WILBUR "BULLET JOE" ROGAN
## OKLAHOMA CITY

**17**

*Courtesy National Baseball Hall of Fame.*

Inducted posthumously into the National Baseball Hall of Fame in 1998, Wilbur "Bullet Joe" Rogan was born in Oklahoma City in 1889. He learned sandlot baseball in northeast Oklahoma City until his family moved to Kansas City at about the time Oklahoma became a state. In 1911, Rogan joined the military and played for Army teams until he was discovered by Casey Stengel.

Because the major leagues were segregated, Stengel suggested Rogan play for the Kansas City Monarchs, the premier team of the Negro Leagues. At age 31, in 1920, Rogan began a remarkable 15-year career with the Monarchs during which he completed 131 of 192 games with a winning percentage of .721. His 151 wins are tops in the Negro Leagues. On days when he was not pitching, Rogan played centerfield and was an outstanding hitter. His lifetime batting average was .343.

# TOMMY McDONALD
## UNIVERSITY OF OKLAHOMA

**18**

McDonald, given the nickname "Blonde Blur," led OU to two national championships in 1955 and 1956. Born in New Mexico, he broke the high school scoring records as a quarterback but was changed to a running back by OU Coach Bud Wilkinson.

McDonald won the Maxwell Award in 1956 as the nation's best collegiate player, was third in the Heisman Trophy balloting, and set an NCAA record for scoring touchdowns in 20 of 21 games as a Sooner. He was also the *Sporting News* Player of the Year in 1956.

*Courtesy Pro Football Hall of Fame.*

In the NFL, McDonald played seven of his 12 seasons for the Philadelphia Eagles. He was selected for the Pro Bowl six times and led the league in touchdown receptions twice. He was the last non-kicker in the NFL to play without a face mask.

McDonald is a member of both the College and Pro Football Halls of Fame. He never played a losing game at OU and had the longest career in the NFL of any OU player in history.

*Courtesy National Baseball Hall of Fame.*

Known as "Big Poison," Waner and his brother Lloyd are the only two brothers enshrined in the National Baseball Hall of Fame. Born in Harrah, Waner played in the Pittsburgh Pirates outfield for 15 seasons and played five more years for the Boston Braves, Brooklyn Dodgers, and New York Yankees.

Waner was the National League MVP in 1927, the same year Babe Ruth hit 60 home runs in the American League. Waner led the National League in batting three times and had more than 3,000 hits in his career. He is tied with Chipper Jones with the most consecutive games with an extra-base hit—14. He had a lifetime batting average of .333 and was inducted into the National Baseball Hall of Fame in 1952. After his retirement as a player, Waner stayed in baseball as a hitting coach until his death in 1965.

# MARK PRICE
## BARTLESVILLE & ENID

# 20

Born in Bartlesville and raised in Enid, Price was the Oklahoma High School Basketball Player of the Year in 1982. He played college basketball at Georgia Tech University where he made the all conference team three times.

During a 12-year career in the NBA, mostly with the Cleveland Cavaliers, he scored more than 10,000 points and is the NBA's best-ever free throw shooter with a career 90.4 percent average. He also made more than 40 percent of attempted three-point shots in his career. He holds the Cleveland team record for assists, free throw percentage, and three-point goals attempted and made. He held the Cavaliers' record for steals until it was surpassed in 2008 by Lebron James.

Price made the NBA All Star team four times and averaged 15.2 points and 6.7 assists per game during his career. He is the brother of OU basketball star Brent Price and the son of Denny Price, a longtime basketball figure in Oklahoma, whose high school single-game state tournament scoring record, 42 points in 1956, was matched by son, Mark, 27 years later.

# JIM SHOULDERS
## HENRYETTA

Shoulders entered and won his first rodeo at age 14. Born and raised near Tulsa, and a graduate of East Central High School, he won his first major rodeo crown at Madison Square Garden in New York City at age 19. Two years later, he won his first Rodeo Cowboy Association (RCA) All-Around Cowboy award and used his winnings to buy a ranch near Henryetta.

One of the most famous all-time rodeo champions, Shoulders had an unequaled record of 16 RCA championships from 1949 to 1959. His 16 world championships include five All-Around Cowboy awards, seven Bull Rider awards, and four Bareback Rider awards. He was tough and suffered a string of injuries. Rodeo announcer Clem McSpadden said, "If there was ever a man who had no pain quotient, it was him."

Shoulders died in 2007. He is the only cowboy in the Madison Square Garden Hall of Fame.

# NANCY LOPEZ
## UNIVERSITY OF TULSA

**22**

Lopez is the only woman golfer to win the LPGA Rookie of the Year, Player of the Year, and the Vare Trophy for lowest scoring average for the same season, 1978. She was born in California but played two years of college golf at the University of Tulsa. She left college after her sophomore year and turned professional in 1977 after she won the individual title of the Association of Intercollegiate Athletics for Women (AIAW) before the NCAA sanctioned a national championships in women's golf.

In 1978, her first full year as a pro, Lopez won nine tournaments, including five in a row. She appeared on the cover of *Sports Illustrated* and was named the Associated Press Female Athlete of the Year. She also won that honor in 1985. She was LPGA Player of the Year four times, the LPGA Tour Money Winner three times, and won the Vare Trophy three times. She was a member of the United States Solheim Cup team in 1990 and captain of the team in 2005. With 50 tournament wins in her LPGA career, she is a member of the World Golf Hall of Fame.

# MARQUES HAYNES
## SAND SPRINGS & LANGSTON UNIVERSITY

**23**

*Courtesy Oklahoma Hall of Fame.*

Haynes, best known as the "World's Greatest Dribbler," perhaps played more professional basketball games than anyone in history. He grew up in Sand Springs and led Booker T. Washington High School to the state basketball championship in 1942. He played at Langston University where his team posted a 112-2 record, including a rare win over the Harlem Globetrotters.

From 1947 to 1953, Haynes toured with the Globetrotters in a starring role with Goose Tatum. Haynes could bounce the ball three times a second and maintain the dribble one inch off the floor. In his prime, he turned down the chance to become the second-highest-paid player in the NBA. Instead, he founded his own barnstorming team, the Harlem Magicians. In 1992, he retired after 46 years in professional basketball. In 1998, he was elected to the National Basketball Hall of Fame and in 2011 was inducted into the Oklahoma Hall of Fame.

# THURMAN THOMAS

## OKLAHOMA STATE UNIVERSITY

**24**

In 2009, Thomas was eighth all time in the NFL for yards from scrimmage, rushing and passing, one spot ahead of Tony Dorsett. A Texas native, Thomas rushed for 4,595 yards at OSU and was consensus All American in 1985 and Big Eight Conference Offensive Player of the Year in 1985 and 1987. Thomas' jersey has been retired at OSU. He is the school's all time leading rusher.

A member of both the College and Pro Football Halls of Fame, Thomas played 13 seasons in the NFL, all but the last year with the Buffalo Bills where he is the leading career rusher and second-leading receiver. A five-time Pro Bowl selection, he was the NFL MVP in 1991. He is one of only three pro football running backs to have more than 400 career receptions and more than 10,000 yards rushing. He was selected as a member of the NFL 1990s All-Decade Team.

*Courtesy Pro Football Hall of Fame.*

Born and raised in Japan, Uetake won three NCAA championships as a college wrester at OSU. Called a "TokyOkie," he competed in the Olympics as a member of the Japanese team and won the Bantamweight gold medal in the 1964 games in Tokyo and at Mexico City in 1968.

In 1972, Uetake returned to Stillwater as coach of the Japanese team and received a four-minute standing ovation.

## ALLIE REYNOLDS
### OKLAHOMA CITY & OKLAHOMA STATE UNIVERSITY

# 26

"Super Chief" was born in Bethany but was a star athlete at Oklahoma City Capitol High School. He played college baseball and football at Oklahoma A & M, now Oklahoma State University, where the baseball field is named for him.

Reynolds spent 13 stellar years in the major leagues for the Cleveland Indians and New York Yankees. It was as a Yankee that he won the status as the best big-game pitcher of his time. He pitched on six world championship teams in eight seasons in New York.

In 1952, Reynolds was the first American League pitcher to post two no-hitters in a single season. The soft-spoken hurler was proud of his Creek Indian heritage and founded Red Earth, an annual celebration of Native American culture in Oklahoma City.

Reynolds may have been the best World Series pitcher ever. From 1949 to 1953, when New York won five consecutive world championships, he was 7-2 with a 2.79 earned run average in World Series games. He is second in career World Series wins and saves. He died in Oklahoma City in 1994.

# RUSSELL WESTBROOK
## OKLAHOMA CITY THUNDER

**27**

Born in Long Beach, California, Westbrook played college basketball at UCLA where he was Pac-10 Defensive Player of the Year in 2008. He skipped his final college season to enter the 2008 NBA draft. He was selected as the fourth overall pick by the Seattle SuperSonics that moved to Oklahoma City six days after the draft.

Westbrook is a three-time NBA All-Star, was a member of the American gold medal winning team in the 2012 Olympic Games, and has become well-known in the NBA for his aggressive play and taking the ball to the bucket. A knee injury slowed him during the 2012 NBA Finals and for part of the 2013-2014 season.

# SEAN O'GRADY
## OKLAHOMA CITY

# 28

O'Grady, the only world champion boxer from Oklahoma, was born in Texas but moved with his family to Oklahoma City at age 11. He began boxing as a teenager, managed by his father, boxing promoter Pat O'Grady.

O'Grady won the United States Boxing Association lightweight title in 1980 and the World Boxing Association lightweight championship in 1981. He retired from boxing in 1983 with 81 wins—70 by knockout—and five losses. He began a successful career as a commercial real estate broker, boxing coach and promoter, and television boxing analyst for ESPN, CBS, USA Network, and Fox.

Berning was the first woman golfer to receive a scholarship at Oklahoma City University, but had to play on the men's team because OCU had no women's squad. By college, she was already an excellent golfer, mentored by legendary Lincoln Park golf pro U.C. Ferguson.

After graduating from OCU with a business degree, Berning joined the LPGA in 1964 and won Rookie of the Year honors. She also won five tournaments. She is one of only three women to win the U.S. Open three times and one of four lady golfers to win the Open in back-to-back years. She was inducted

into the National Golf Coaches Association Hall of Fame in 1986. After retirement from the LPGA, Berning became a respected golf teaching professional.

## 30

# ALVAN ADAMS
## OKLAHOMA CITY &
## UNIVERSITY OF OKLAHOMA

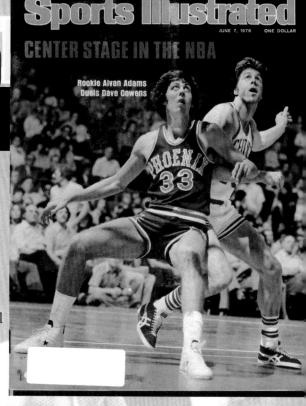

Known as the "Oklahoma Kid," Adams was a basketball star at Putnam City High School where he led his team to the Class 4A state title and earned National High School Player of the Year honors in 1972. For college, he picked OU over UCLA, Maryland, and Kansas. As a Sooner, he set a number of new records such as most points in a game, 43, and the most rebounds in a game, 28. He was an All American and the only unanimous selection on the Big Eight Conference 1970s All-Decade Team. He was named MVP of the Big Eight Tournament in each of his three seasons at OU.

Adams bypassed his senior year and was drafted by the Phoenix Suns of the NBA. He had a monster rookie season, averaging 19 points, 9.1 rebounds, and 5.6 assists per game. In 13 pro seasons with the Suns, he scored 13,910 points. He ranks near the top in Phoenix NBA history in rebounds, assists, steals, and total games. He averaged 4.1 assists per game in his career, third for centers in NBA history to Wilt Chamberlain and Bill Russell.

Adams is one of only three OU basketball players to have their numbers retired. After his retirement, he became director of operations for the America West Arena in Phoenix and events coordinator for the Suns.

*Courtesy Oklahoma Hall of Fame.*

# WAYMAN TISDALE
## TULSA & UNIVERSITY OF OKLAHOMA

**31**

Growing up in Tulsa, Tisdale was influenced by music at his father's church and by basketball from his older brothers. By the eighth grade, he learned to dunk and began to dominate any basketball game in which he was involved. After graduating from Tulsa's Booker T. Washington High School, Tisdale chose OU for college. Coach Billy Tubbs had to reschedule Sunday practices to allow Tisdale the opportunity to play the bass guitar at his Tulsa church on Sunday mornings.

At OU, Tisdale was a three-time Big Eight Conference Player of the Year and the first player in collegiate history to be named first-team All American in his freshman, sophomore, and junior seasons. He still holds the OU record for most points scored after his first, second, and third seasons and for his career. He won a gold medal as a member of the 1984 United States Olympic team.

As a power forward and center, Tisdale averaged more than 15 points and six rebounds per game in a 12-year NBA career with Indiana, Sacramento, and Phoenix. His best season was 1989-1990 when he averaged 22.3 points and 7.5 rebounds per game. In 1997, he became the first OU player to have his jersey number retired, but when Blake Griffin was granted permission to wear the number 23, it came with Tisdale's blessing.

During his NBA career, Tisdale began a successful career as a jazz musician. His albums reached the Top Ten on *Billboard* Magazine's Contemporary Jazz chart. In 2009, Tisdale died after losing his battle with cancer.

# 32

## MARK SCHULTZ
### UNIVERSITY OF OKLAHOMA

A member of the National Wrestling Hall of Fame, Schultz began competitive wrestling his senior year in high school in his native California and won the state championship. He originally chose UCLA for college, but transferred with his older brother, David, to OU.

In 1981, Schultz won the NCAA championship at 167 pounds and repeated the feat the following two years at 177 pounds. In 1984 at the Olympic Games in Los Angeles, he became the first American wrestler in 52 years to cap three NCAA titles with the gold medal in freestyle. He won four national freestyle titles, two world championships, and a Pan American gold medal. After several years as a collegiate coaching assistant, Schultz became head wrestling coach at Brigham Young University.

## BILLY SIMS
### UNIVERSITY OF OKLAHOMA

**33**

Sims rushed for more than 100 yards every game of his high school career in his hometown of Hooks, Texas. Recruited by OU, he started off slowly, behind running backs like Joe Washington. By 1978, however, he rushed for 1,762 yards and 20 touchdowns, leading the nation in rushing and scoring. He was unanimous All American, MVP in the Orange Bowl, and won the Heisman Trophy. He finished his collegiate career in 1979 by again leading the nation in scoring.

Sims was the top overall pick in the 1980 NFL draft by the Detroit Lions. He played five seasons in Detroit, going to the Pro Bowl three seasons. He was Rookie of the Year in the NFL in 1980 and rushed for more than 1,000 yards in his first two seasons, but was prevented from continuing his streak by the NFL strike in 1982.

Sims blew out his knee while making a cut in 1984. Unable to restore his strength, he retired, ending a brilliant career in professional football that lasted less than five years.

# KENNY MONDAY
## TULSA & OKLAHOMA STATE UNIVERSITY

**34**

Monday was born in Tulsa and was a four-time state champion wrestler at Tulsa's Booker T. Washington High School. He never lost a match from the seventh grade through high school, with a record of 140-0-1.

At OSU, Monday was a three-time All American. He won the NCAA title in 1984 at 150 pounds. His college record of 121-12-2 helped the Cowboys win two Big Eight titles. Monday won the gold medal in Freestyle at

the 1988 Seoul Olympics and the silver medal in Freestyle at the 1992 Olympics in Barcelona. He also won the 1989 World Championship and a series of United States Freestyle titles in 1985, 1988, 1991, and 1996.

Monday is a member of the National Wrestling Hall of Fame.

*Courtesy Oklahoma Hall of Fame.*

# BLAKE GRIFFIN 35
## OKLAHOMA CITY & UNIVERSITY OF OKLAHOMA

Griffin was born in Oklahoma City and played high school basketball for his father and coach, Tommy Griffin, at Oklahoma Christian School. He played college basketball at OU and was the consensus National Player of the Year in his sophomore season in 2009. He also was consensus first-team All American.

Griffin was selected as the first overall pick in the 2009 NBA draft by the Los Angeles Clippers, but missed his first year with a kneecap injury. As a rookie in 2011, he was NBA Rookie of the Year and won the Slam Dunk Contest. He is a four-time NBA All-Star and has helped propel the Clippers from a second division team to a perennial playoff contender.

# SPEC SANDERS
## TEMPLE

# 36

Sanders was born in Temple, Oklahoma, and was a substitute football player at the University of Texas. However, he was the sixth overall draft pick in the 1942 NFL draft, taken by the Washington Redskins. He never played for the Redskins because of Navy service during World War II.

After the war, Sanders played for the New York Yankees of the NFL-rival All American Football Conference (AAFC) from 1946 to 1949. He led the AAFC in rushing in 1946 and 1947. In 1950, he played for the New York Yanks of the NFL, was named to the Pro Bowl, and led the league in interceptions.

# CRYSTAL ROBINSON
## ATOKA & SOUTHEASTERN OKLAHOMA STATE UNIVERSITY

**37**

*Courtesy Fleer - Skybox International, LP.*

Born in Atoka, Robinson starred at Southeastern Oklahoma State University in Durant and was only the third women's basketball player ever inducted in the NAIA Hall of Fame. She was chosen a member of *The Daily Oklahoman* All-Century team of both high school and college players.

After being named the American Basketball League Rookie of the Year in 1996, Robinson jumped to the WNBA in 1999 and signed with the New York Liberty. She played for the Washington Mystics until her retirement in 2007 to become an assistant coach for the Mystics.

# CHARLES COE
## ARDMORE & UNIVERSITY OF OKLAHOMA

**38**

Coe was perhaps the best amateur golfer in American sports history. He was born in Ardmore and was the star of the golf team at OU, winning the Big Seven championship in his three seasons as a Sooner.

Coe never turned pro, opting instead to spend time with his business and family. He won the U.S. Amateur championship in 1949 and 1958. The following year, he was runner-up to Jack Nicklaus. He was on the U.S. Walker Cup team seven times and played on the America's Cup team six times. He was the best amateur in the 1958 U.S. Open. In 1961, he was the last amateur to threaten to win the Masters Tournament. He "lipped" a 25-foot putt on the 18th hole that would have forced Gary Player into a playoff. He holds nearly every record for an amateur in the Masters.

A successful oil man in Oklahoma City after his retirement from competition in 1970, Coe died in 2001. The golf center at OU is named for him.

# HUBERT "GEESE" AUSBIE
## CRESCENT

**39**

One of the most beloved and talented Harlem Globetrotters of all time, Ausbie was born in Crescent. He attended Douglass High School in Crescent, scoring 70, 54, and 62 points in three consecutive games during a tournament. More than 200 colleges recruited him, but he attended Philander Smith College in Little Rock, Arkansas. In his junior season he was the third-highest scorer in the nation, trailing only Elgin Baylor of Seattle and Oscar Robertson of Cincinnati.

After college, Ausbie chose to play for the Harlem Globetrotters, a more lucrative professional career than in the NBA. He starred for the Globetrotters from 1961 to 1985, playing before 100 million fans in more than 100 countries on six continents. After the retirement of Meadowlark Lemon, Ausbie assumed the role as "The Clown Prince of Basketball." Ausbie returned to the Globetrotters in 1995 as coach and director of operations.

# CARL MAYS
## KINGFISHER

**40**

Raised in Kingfisher after his parents moved to Oklahoma Territory from his native Kentucky, Mays was one of the best right-handed pitchers in baseball from 1916 to 1926. However, he is best remembered for throwing the pitch at Yankee Stadium that struck Cleveland Indian Ray Chapmen in 1920. Chapman died the next day in a New York City hospital.

Mays won 207 major league games for the Boston Red Sox, New York Yankees, Cincinnati Reds, and New York Giants from 1915 to 1929. He played on four world championship clubs, led the American League in wins in 1921, was a two-time American League

*Courtesy National Baseball Hall of Fame.*

complete game and shutout leader, and had five seasons with 20 or more wins. He is the only Red Sox pitcher to toss two nine-inning complete victories on the same day, beating the Philadelphia Athletics on August 30, 1918. He died in 1971.

## DOLL HARRIS
### CEMENT
**41**

Raised in Cement, Harris scored 19 points in the title game for the Oklahoma Presbyterian College Cardinals who won the national AAU women's basketball championship in 1932. The Lady Cardinals set a world record of 89 consecutive wins against the toughest competition of their time. The Durant, Oklahoma school won two national championships, one North American championship, and the 1933 Women's World

*Courtesy Oklahoma Sports Hall of Fame.*

Championship. In the 1932 AAU title game, Harris outplayed Mildred "Babe" Didricksen, the star of the Dallas Golden Cyclones.

## CHRIS PAUL
### OKLAHOMA CITY

42

Paul, a North Carolina native and basketball star at Wake Forest University, was Oklahoma's first major league superstar. He was drafted in 2005 by the New Orleans Hornets who were uprooted by Hurricane Katrina and made their home for two seasons in Oklahoma City's Ford Center.

Paul was NBA Rookie of the Year in 2006 and led the Hornets to the second round of the NBA Playoffs. He also won a gold medal as a member of the United States Olympic basketball team.

Paul had a solid sophomore season, much to the delight of his admiring Oklahoma fans. In 2011, he was traded to the Los Angeles Clippers and has become one of the NBA's best point guards.

## ACE GUTOWSKY
### KINGFISHER & OKLHOMA CITY UNIVERSITY

**43**

When he retired from professional football in 1939, Gutowsky was the career leading rusher in the NFL. He was born in Russia but raised in Kingfisher.

He played football at Oklahoma City University before being signed by the Portsmouth Spartans of the NFL in 1932 where he played for two seasons. The Portsmouth franchise was later moved to Detroit, Michigan, and became the Lions. Gutowsky was the top running back for the Lions until 1938. He was part of the Lions' 1935 NFL championship team.

Gutowsky played his final season for the Brooklyn Dodgers, which later became the New York Yanks and Dallas Texans. He died in 1976 in Oklahoma City and is buried in Kingfisher.

# IRA DAVENPORT
## TONKAWA

**44**

Davenport, running for University Prep School of Tonkawa, clocked an amazing 9.8 seconds in the 100-yard dash in the 1908 OU Interscholastics, a state record that stood for 26 years. He swept the 100-, 220-, and 440-yard dashes at a national high school track meet in 1908.

At the 1912 Olympic Games in Stockholm, Sweden, Davenport won the bronze medal in the 800 meters in a blanket 1-2-3 American finish in which all three runners broke the world record. As a student at the University of Chicago, he was Big Ten Conference champion three times in the 440- and 880-yard runs.

*Opening ceremonies at the 1912 Olympic Games in Stockholm, Sweden.*

## MAT HOFFMAN
### EDMOND
**45**

At age 11, Hoffman entered the freestyle BMX circuit as an amateur. At age 16, he was the youngest professional rider in the sport. He revolutionized the sport and is considered one of the best vertical ramp riders in BMX history and has "invented" many of the sport's tricks. He was listed in the 2004 *Guinness Book of World Records* for jumping more than 50 feet above the ground. He won the bronze medal at the 2001 X Games and the silver medal at the 2002 X Games.

A successful promoter of BMX Freestyle, Hoffman was elected president of the International BMX Freestyle Federation, the governing body of the sport, in 2005.

# BOBBY BOYD

## 46

### UNIVERSITY OF OKLAHOMA

Boyd was born in Dallas, Texas, but chose to play college football at OU where he was quarterback for Bud Wilkinson's Sooners. In 1960 he was the 119th pick of the NFL draft in the tenth round. He surprised football experts by becoming a star for the Baltimore Colts from 1960 to 1968.

Boyd made the Pro Bowl in 1964 and 1968 and was named to the NFL 1960s All-Decade Team. He led the NFL with nine interceptions in 1965. He holds the Colts' franchise record of career interceptions with 57. He has been retired for more than 40 years, but in 2009, was still ranked tenth in the NFL in career interceptions.

*Courtesy The Topps Company, Inc.*

**47**

Born in Chickasha, McCracken was officially designated the greatest amateur basketball player in history by the Amateur Athletic Union (AAU). He played basketball for Coach Henry Iba at Classen High School in Oklahoma City and at Northwest Missouri State Teachers College.

After college, McCracken, known as "Jumping Jack," opted to bypass professional basketball and instead play for the Denver, Colorado team in the AAU. He died at age 46 in 1948.

Williams, a California native, was a starter on the undefeated 2000 OU national championship football team. He set a school record for tackles for loss by a defensive back. In 2001, his junior season, Williams won the Bronko Nagurski Trophy as the nation's top defensive player and the Jim Thorpe Award as the nation's top defensive back. A two-time All American, he was the eighth overall pick in the 2002 NFL draft.

Williams spent the first seven seasons of his professional career playing in the defensive backfield for the Dallas Cowboys. He often employed the horse-collar tackle to down opposing players, resulting in the NFL rule, called the "Roy Williams Rule," that bans such tackles. After the 2007 season, Williams was named to the Pro Bowl for the fifth consecutive year. He played his final two seasons in the NFL for the Cincinnati Bengals.

## LLOYD WANER
### HARRAH

**49**

The younger brother of the famous Waners of Harrah, Lloyd, known as "Little Poison," was elected to the National Baseball Hall of Fame in 1967. The Waners were discovered by a major league scout while playing for the town team in Ada. Lloyd played for East Central State College before signing a professional contract.

At only 5'8" and 142 pounds, Lloyd batted over .300 in 12 of his 20 seasons in the major leagues as a Pittsburgh Pirate. His lifetime batting average was .316, with a high of .362 in 1930. In 1927, as a rookie, Lloyd led the National League with 133 runs scored and was third in batting behind his brother who won the crown. He also set the major league record for most hits in a rookie season, 223, a rare baseball record that may never be broken.

During World War II, Lloyd returned to Oklahoma City and worked at the Douglass Aircraft plant. After retirement as a player, he scouted for the Pirates and Orioles and was a foreman for the City of Oklahoma City. He died in 1982.

*Courtesy National Baseball Hall of Fame.*

# DENNIS RODMAN **50**
## SOUTHEASTERN OKLAHOMA STATE UNIVERSITY

Born in New Jersey and raised in one of the poorest sections of Dallas, Texas, Rodman played college basketball at Southeastern Oklahoma State University in Durant. He was a three-time NAIA All American and led the nation in rebounding twice. He averaged more than 25 points per game for his NAIA career. At a pre-draft camp after college, he caught the eye of the Detroit Pistons.

Entering the 1986 NBA draft, Rodman was selected in the second round by the Pistons and joined a rugged team of "bad boys."

Rodman fit well into the team and became notorious for presenting himself with many piercings and tattoos. He wore a wedding dress to promote the release of his autobiography.

In 15 years in the NBA for the Pistons, San Antonio Spurs, Chicago Bulls, Los Angeles Lakers, and Dallas Mavericks, Rodman earned All-Defensive First Team honors seven times and was voted the league's Defensive Player of the Year twice. He led the NBA in rebounds per game for a record seven consecutive years and won five NBA championships. He is the number 12 rebounder in NBA history.

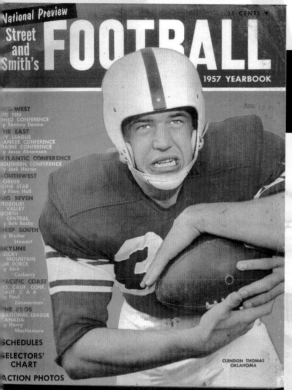

## CLENDON THOMAS
### OKLAHOMA CITY & UNIVERSITY OF OKLAHOMA

**51**

In 1963, Thomas was the highest paid defensive back in the NFL with a whopping salary of $35,000. Born in Oklahoma City, he was an outstanding player at Southeast High School. He helped lead the OU Sooners to back-to-back national championships in 1955 and 1956. In his junior year he led the nation in scoring as a halfback with 18 touchdowns. He was a consensus All American in his senior season and finished ninth in the Heisman Trophy balloting. In his final home game, Thomas broke the OU record for touchdowns and career rushing.

In the 1958 NFL draft, Thomas was selected in the second round by the Los Angeles Rams. He played defensive back for Los Angeles for four years before being traded to the Pittsburgh Steelers for his final seven years in the NFL.

# DANNY HODGE
## PERRY & UNIVERSITY OF OKLAHOMA

**52**

One of Oklahoma's most famous wrestlers, Hodge showed his great strength in 2006 on ESPN by crushing an apple with one hand. He was a winner at Perry High School before he joined the Navy and competed as an Olympian. He won the silver medal in men's Freestyle at the 1956 Olympics at Melbourne, Australia.

As a college wrestler at OU, Hodge won three NCAA titles, three Big Seven Conference championships, and was never knocked from a standing position in winning all 46 of his collegiate bouts. He was selected as the NCAA's Outstanding Wrestler in 1956 and 1957. He is the only amateur wrestler to ever appear on the cover of *Sports Illustrated*.

Hodge made his debut as a professional wrestler in 1959. He worked in that profession for 18 years and was a five-time USA Tag Team Champion.

The Dan Hodge Trophy, the equivalent of the Heisman Trophy in amateur wrestling, is named for him. He was a charter member of the National Wrestling Hall of Fame.

A native of Arkansas, O'Neal was a defensive star and two-time All American at OSU before becoming the eighth overall pick in the 1986 NFL draft. He played the first ten of his 13 NFL seasons with the San Diego Chargers, completing his career with the St. Louis Rams and Kansas City Chiefs.

In 1986, O'Neal was the NFL Defensive Rookie of the Year. He was selected for the Pro Bowl six times. He is tied for seventh place on the all-time NFL sacks list.

# GREG PRUITT

**UNIVERSITY OF OKLAHOMA**

## 54

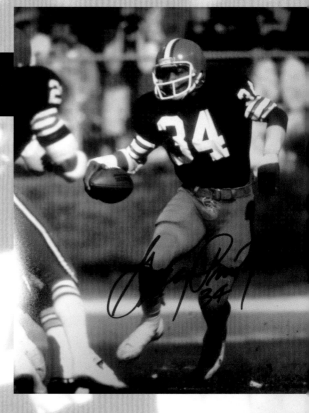

Another in a line of Texas running backs to choose OU at which to play college football, Pruitt earned consensus All American honors as a halfback for the Sooners in 1971 and 1972. He still owns the school record for most yards in a game with 294 against Kansas State in 1971. His 9.41 yards per rushing attempt in 1971 is an NCAA record. At OU, he rushed for 1,665 yards as a junior, but injuries kept him 62 yards short of another 1,000-yard season in 1972. His college record earned him a spot in the College Football Hall of Fame and the Helms Foundation Football Hall of Fame.

In 1973, Pruitt was a second-round draft choice of the Cleveland Browns where he starred until 1981 when he was traded to the Los Angeles Raiders for his final three seasons in the NFL. He gained more than 1,000 yards in three consecutive seasons and was selected for three Pro Bowls. Pruitt purposely wore thin jerseys that ripped apart in the hands of would-be tacklers, resulting in the passage of the Greg Pruitt Rule in the NFL.

Dial was born in Marlow, Oklahoma, and was a track and field star at OSU. He is best known for winning the bronze medal in pole vault at the 1989 World Indoor Championships in Budapest, Hungary. He set a world indoor pole vaulting record at 5.96 meters in Norman in June, 1987.

When he retired from active participation, Dial turned to coaching. In 1993, he was named head coach of the men's and women's track and cross country programs at Oral Roberts University. He was named to the OSU Hall of Fame in 2002 and has coached more than 20 All American track and field stars at ORU.

# JOE WASHINGTON
## UNIVERSITY OF OKLAHOMA

**56**

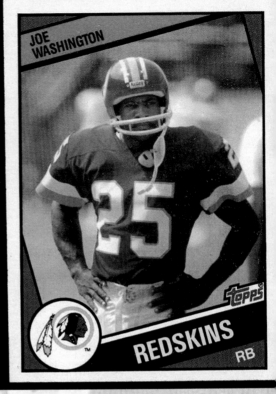

*Courtesy The Topps Company Inc.*

"Little Joe" was a Parade football All American in his hometown of Port Arthur, Texas, where his father was his coach. At OU, he was a two-time first-team All American and finished third in the Heisman Trophy vote in 1974 and fifth in 1975. Coach Barry Switzer said Washington was "the purest runner" OU ever had. As a Sooner, Washington gained 4,071 yards and was a member of two national championship teams. He is a member of the College Football Hall of Fame.

Drafted as the fourth pick of the 1976 NFL draft, he began his pro career with the San Diego Chargers. He was traded to the Baltimore Colts in 1978. He is remembered for one of the greatest individual performances on Monday Night Football. Against the Patriots, Washington scored or helped score the Colts' final three touchdowns in a game that saw 41 fourth quarter points. He caught a touchdown pass, threw an option pass for another score, and won the game on a 96-yard kickoff return for a touchdown.

Washington played in two Super Bowls. He is the only Washington Redskin to lead the team in both rushing and receiving in the same season. In his ten-year pro career, he gained 4,839 yards on the ground and caught 395 passes for 3,412 yards.

# DAVE SCHULTZ
## OKLAHOMA STATE UNIVERSITY & UNIVERSITY OF OKLAHOMA

Schultz, born in California, is the only wrestler to be named All American at both OU and OSU. His senior year is considered by most experts as the most successful senior year in high school in American wrestling history.

Schultz was All American at OSU for his first two years of college before transferring to OU. In 1982, he won the NCAA championship at 167 pounds, ironically, defeating a former teammate from OSU, Mike Sheets.

In addition to winning the gold medal in freestyle at the 1984 Los Angeles Olympic Games, Schultz won one gold, three silver, and two bronze medals in World Championship Freestyle competition. He also won the bronze medal in the 1995 Pan American Games. He won ten Senior National titles in 19 years at three weight divisions. He is the only American to win the prestigious tournament in Tbilisi, Georgia, twice.

In 1996, Schultz was shot to death while coaching the private Team Foxcatcher squad. Team owner, John E. du Pont was found guilty of the crime.

## JON KOLB
**OWASSO & OKLAHOMA STATE UNIVERSITY**

**58**

Born in Ponca City, Kolb was an All-State football star at Owasso High School before enrolling at OSU where he was an outstanding center. He was named All Big Eight twice and was an All American in 1968. He was selected in the third round of the NFL draft by the Pittsburgh Steelers in 1969.

Kolb was a solid starter for the Steelers for 13 seasons. He started at tackle in 177 games and earned four Super Bowl rings. He was considered one of the NFL's strongest offensive lineman, protecting quarterback Terry Bradshaw's blind side and opening holes for running backs Franco Harris and Rocky Bleier.

After retirement as a player, Kolb became the Steelers' strength and conditioning coach. He has released more than 50 exercise videos.

**59**

Born in Oklahoma City, Murcer was an all-around athlete at Southeast High School. He batted .458 with only one strikeout in his senior year and caught the attention of New York Yankees scout Tom Greenwade who had previously signed Mickey Mantle for the Yankees.

Ironically, Murcer replaced Mantle, his childhood hero, in centerfield in New York. Murcer played 19 major league seasons, primarily with the Yankees, although he spent four seasons with the San Francisco Giants and Chicago Cubs.

Murcer shares the major league record of hitting four consecutive home runs. He was an All-Star selection five times from 1971 to 1975. He won the Gold Glove for outfielders in 1972 and led the American League in runs, extra-base hits, and total bases. In his career, Murcer had a career .277 batting average with 252 home runs and 1,043 runs batted in. He was only the third New York Yankee to earn $100,000 per season, after Joe DiMaggio and Mantle. At age 26, he was the youngest player of his time to earn $100,000.

After his active playing days, Murcer was president of the Oklahoma City 89ers minor league franchise and a beloved Yankees broadcaster for many years. He died of cancer in 2008.

# EASY JET
## SAYRE

**60**

Easy Jet was born an American Quarter Horse in 1967 on a ranch near Sayre owned by Walter Merrick. Two years later, he won the All American Futurity, the highest race for quarter horses and was named the World Champion Quarter Race Horse. In two years of racing, Easy Jet won 27 of 38 races, then retired from the race track to become a breeding stallion.

Easy Jet is one of only two horses to be a member and his offspring to be a member of the American Quarter Horse Association Hall of Fame. He was the first quarter horse to sire an All American Futurity Winner, the first of three winners of that race. He also fathered nine Champion Quarter Running Horses.

Easy Jet's ownership and breeding rights were ultimately valued at $30 million, 60 shares worth $500,000 each. He died in 1992. By the following year, his foals had earned more than $25 million on the race track.

---

# EASY JET

*With a big heart and blistering speed, Easy Jet earned a spot among the legendary figures of the Quarter Horse world.*

The sorrel stallion was born in 1967 and was a product of Walter Merrick's breeding program. Easy Jet was sired by the phenomenal Jet Deck and out of the Thoroughbred mare Lena's Bar (TB) by Three Bars (TB).

Once broke to ride, the sorrel was worked against Jet Smooth at 350 yards and won. Merrick decided to run Easy Jet in a yearling race at Blue Ribbon Downs in Sallisaw, Oklahoma. The big colt won with daylight between him and the second-place horse.

This was the beginning of an illustrious racing career. The Oklahoma rancher sent Easy Jet to the starting gates 26 times as a 2-year-old. The sorrel won 22 times, including the All-American, Kansas and Sunland Fall futurities.

In 1969, Easy Jet was the racing world champion. The sorrel returned in 1970, and was the racing champion stallion.

In 1971, Merrick sold half interest in Easy Jet to Joe McDermott. Over the next several years, Easy Jet was sold several different times. The Buena Suerte Ranch in Roswell, New Mexico, bought Easy Jet for $3.5 million, and in the early '80s the stallion was syndicated for $30,000,000. Easy Jet's last owners were Merrick and Mark and Bill Allen.

Easy Jet's first foals hit the ground in 1971, and by 1973, he was on the AQHA leading sires list. Some of the sorrel's champion get include Easy Date, Pie In The Sky, My Easy Credit, Easy Angel, Easily Smashed, Extra Easy and Megahertz.

Easy Jet was standing at the Lazy E in Guthrie, Oklahoma, in 1992 when it was decided he needed to be euthanized.

Easy Jet died in 1992 at 25, and was inducted into the American Quarter Horse Hall of Fame in 1993.

**INDUCTED INTO THE AMERICAN QUARTER HORSE** *Hall of Fame* **1993**

Born in Oklahoma City and a star athlete at Millwood High School, Carter is remembered best for hitting a walk-off home run off the Phillies Mitch Williams to win the World Series in 1993 for the Toronto Blue Jays. Carter played college baseball at Wichita State University. He was *The Sporting News* College Player of the Year in 1981 and was selected as the second overall pick in that year's baseball draft.

In 16 major leagues seasons, he hit 396 home runs. He was just the tenth player in history to reach the 300-home run plateau and steal 200 bases. He left Toronto in 1997 as the Blue

Jay's all-time homerun leader. He played for six teams in the major league, but his longest stretch was with the Blue Jays from 1991 to 1997. Carter was an All Star selection five times and was on two world championship clubs.

# JIM BARNES
## STILLWATER

**62**

Born in Arkansas, but raised in Stillwater, Barnes played college basketball for the Cameron Junior College Aggies in Lawton and the University of Texas at El Paso. He was the top pick in the 1964 NBA draft, selected by the New York Knicks. He also was a member of the American Olympic basketball team that won the gold medal in the 1964 Olympics in Tokyo, Japan.

Barnes was named to the 1965 NBA All-rookie Team. Known as "Bad News" Barnes, he played seven seasons in the NBA with five teams, scoring 3,997 career points. He retired in 1971 and died in 2002.

His real name was John Leonard Roosevelt Martin, born in Temple, Oklahoma. He learned baseball on the sandlots of Oklahoma City and sold soft drinks at the old Western League ball park. He played at Ardmore and Guthrie in the minor leagues before becoming one of the most aggressive major league players ever as a member of the St. Louis Cardinals' Gashouse Gang.

Martin was the first batter in the first baseball All Star game in 1933. He lived up to his nickname "Pepper." He dashed for every base, often ending the run with an artistic belly flop slide. Once asked how he learned to run so fast, he said, "I grew up in Oklahoma. Out there, once you start runnin', there ain't nothing to stop you."

Martin dominated the 1931 World Series. He batted .500 with five stolen bases and five extra-base hits. He was so popular, a five-chapter series, "The Life of Pepper Martin," began running in the nation's newspapers the day after the Series ended. For his exploits in the World Series, he was named the male athlete of the year by the Associated Press. He has the third highest World Series career batting average. Martin died in 1965 in McAlester.

# RALPH NEELY 64
## UNIVERSITY OF OKLAHOMA

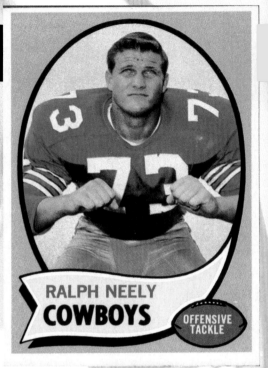

RALPH NEELY
**COWBOYS**

OFFENSIVE TACKLE

*Courtesy The Topps Company Inc.*

Neely was born in Arkansas and grew up in New Mexico before choosing to play college football for Coach Bud Wilkinson at OU. As a Sooner, Neely was an All American his senior year at offensive tackle.

Neely was drafted in the second round of the NFL draft in 1965 by the Baltimore Colts and by the Houston Oilers in the American Football League draft. Wanting to stay to close to home, he secretly signed a contract with the Oilers. When that fact was known, he and two other OU players were suspended from the 1965 Gator Bowl. Neely changed his mind when he discovered that the Colts sold their draft rights to the Dallas Cowboys. He sent his signing check back to the Oilers and signed with the Cowboys.

Neely was All-Pro four times in 13 seasons as a dominant offensive lineman. Selected as a member of the NFL 1960s All-Decade team, he retired after the Cowboys won Super Bowl XII.

# MICHELE SMITH
## OKLAHOMA STATE UNIVERSITY

**65**

A New Jersey native, Smith began playing softball at age five and began pitching at age 15. She is considered by some to be one of the best softball players in history. After a stellar high school career, she brought her pitching talent to Stillwater and the OSU Cowgirls.

Smith's career for Team USA began in 1990 when she was a first-team All American. In the International Softball Federation tournament that year, she pitched a perfect game and was named the MVP of the championship.

Smith won gold medals as a member of the United States National Team in the 1996, 2000, and 2004 Olympic games. A celebrity in her sport, she appeared on "Oprah," CNN, and "NBC's Today Show." She also was a softball analyst for ESPN. After college, Smith became a softball star in Japan. The first foreigner to be featured on the face of the Japanese softball magazine, she was named MVP in the Japanese Professional Softball League seven times. In 2006, she was inducted into the American Softball Association Hall of Fame.

# KENDALL CROSS

## MUSTANG & OKLAHOMA STATE UNIVERSITY

**66**

In high school at Mustang, Cross, a native of Montana, won a state wrestling championship. At OSU, he was a three-time All American and won a NCAA championship in 1989. After graduating from OSU in political science and economics, he worked for Merrill Lynch and trained for the Olympics. He won the gold medal in freestyle at the 1996 Olympic Games in Atlanta.

*Kendall Cross*     *LeShawn Charles*

*Courtesy Oklahoma State University.*

In addition to winning the Olympic gold medal, he was a three-time United States National Champion, USA Wrestling's Athlete of the Year, and the World Cup Champion in 1997. He was inducted as a member of the National Wrestling Hall of Fame in 2002.

# MOOKIE BLAYLOCK
### UNIVERSITY OF OKLAHOMA

**67**

A native of Garland, Texas, Blaylock attended Midland Community College before becoming an Oklahoma Sooner. In 1988 he and Stacey King led OU to the NCAA title game.

Blaylock was selected by the New Jersey Nets as the 12th overall pick in the 1989 NBA draft. He was traded to the Atlanta Hawks prior to the 1992 season. In 1999, he was traded to the Golden State Warriors where he completed his 13-year NBA career.

As a push-and-pass point guard, Blaylock was known as a good defensive stopper. He produced more than 200 steals in a season four times and was first-team NBA All-Defensive Team twice. He was selected for the NBA All-Star team in 1994. When he retired in 2002, Blaylock was 7th all-time in career steals per game, 8th in career three-point field goal attempts, and 11th in career steals.

Blaylock joined Oscar Robertson and Magic Johnson as the only NBA players to lead the league in steals in consecutive years.

## KEITH JACKSON
### UNIVERSITY OF OKLAHOMA

**68**

KEITH JACKSON
PHILADELPHIA EAGLES • TE

TOPPS ALL PRO

*Courtesy The Topps Company Inc.*

Born and raised in Little Rock, Jackson was influenced by Coach Barry Switzer to play college football at OU. He was a consensus All American in 1986 and 1987. Primarily a blocker in the run-oriented Sooner offense, Jackson caught just 62 passes for 1,470 yards in four years at OU. For his excellence as a Sooner, he was inducted into the College Football Hall of Fame in 2001.

Jackson was a first-round draft choice of the Philadelphia Eagles in 1988 and immediately set reception records for tight ends in his rookie season. He was Rookie of the Year in *The Sporting News* and was the only rookie on the NFC's Pro Bowl team.

Jackson played nine seasons in the NFL with the Eagles, Miami Dolphins, and Green Bay Packers. Many football experts consider him one of the greatest tight ends to play the game. He won Pro Bowl honors in six of his nine years in the league.

After retirement, Jackson became a radio and television football analyst and motivational speaker.

## STACEY DALES
### UNIVERSITY OF OKLAHOMA

Dales, the first OU women's basketball player to reach 1,700 points, 600 rebounds, and 700 assists, was born in Canada. At OU, she was a two-time All American, was Big 12 Conference Player of the Year in 2001 and 2002, and led the Sooner women to the national championship game. When she completed her college career, she led the Big 12 in career assists.

Dales was drafted third overall in the 2002 WNBA draft by the Washington Mystics, the highest pick for a Canadian-born player. She also played for the Chicago Sky of the WNBA before becoming a popular basketball analyst and a football sideline reporter for ESPN.

# WALT GARRISON

**OKLAHOMA STATE UNIVERSITY**

**70**

Known for his toughness, Garrison once played an entire football game with a broken ankle. Born in Texas, he was lured to OSU with a football scholarship. Moved from defense to offense in his sophomore season, Garrison became a star runner and led the Big Eight Conference in rushing in 1964.

Garrison, a real Cowboy from OSU as a consistent rodeo performer, was overlooked by many teams in the 1966 NFL draft. He was not picked until the fifth round by the Dallas Cowboys where he became a legendary fullback for nine seasons. He retired as the third leading rusher and fourth leading receiver in Dallas history. He appeared twice in the Pro Bowl and was a member of the world champions in Super Bowl VI.

Cowboy quarterback Don Meredith spoke of Garrison's dependability, "If it was third down and you needed four yards, Walt would give you five. And if it was third down and you needed 20 yards, Walt would give you five."

**Sports Illustrated**
NOVEMBER 10, 1969    50 CENTS
THE SCRAMBLE FOR FOOTBALL'S OSCAR

Steve Owens
of Oklahoma

*Courtesy Bob Burke Collection.*

## STEVE OWENS
### MIAMI & UNIVERSITY OF OKLAHOMA

# 71

The 1969 Heisman Trophy winner at OU, Owens hails from Miami, Oklahoma, where he was an All State and All American high school football player. In his collegiate career as a Sooner, he shattered 13 major school records, nine Big Eight Conference marks, and seven NCAA records. In 2009, he still held the NCAA record for 358 carries his Heisman season, for 905 career attempts, and 56 career touchdowns. He was a consensus All American in 1968 and 1969.

A first round draft choice of the Detroit Lions in 1970, Owens played six seasons in the NFL. He was the first Lion to rush for more than 1,000 yards, with 1,035 yards and eight touchdowns in 1971. He was fourth best in rushing in the NFL that year and was selected to the Pro Bowl.

Later Owens served as athletic director at OU.

# ROY DUVALL
## CHECOTAH

**72**

Raised in Checotah, Duvall won the steer wrestling championship three times in competition of the Professional Rodeo Cowboys Association (PRCA). He qualified for the National Finals Rodeo 24 years, last participating in the grueling steer wrestling completion in 1994, at age 52.

Courtesy *Oklahoma Hall of Fame*.

## BART CONNER
### UNIVERSITY OF OKLAHOMA

**73**

Originally from Illinois, Conner is the only American gymnast in history to win gold medals at each level of competition. He was a junior national champion, an elite national champion, a Pan American Games champion, a World Cup champion, a world champion, and Olympic champion.

Conner won the hearts of Americans when he cried on the victory stand after winning two gold medals at the 1984 Olympic Games. He is married to Nadia Comaneci, the queen of Romanian gymnastics who became the first gymnast in Olympic history to score a perfect 10. They own a gymnastics club in Norman and he is co-editor of *International Gymnastics* Magazine. Conner is a member of the United States Olympic, American Gymnastics, and the International Gymnastics Halls of Fame.

**74**

Born in Oregon, Sherk was an outstanding wrestler and football player at OSU. He was All American in wrestling in 1969 and an All Big Eight defensive player on the gridiron. Selected in the second round of the 1970 NFL draft, he played 12 seasons in professional football, all with the Cleveland Browns.

Sherk was picked for the Pro Bowl four consecutive seasons

*Courtesy The Topps Company Inc.*

from 1973 to 1976 and was the NFL Defensive Player of the Year in 1976. He was a starter from his rookie season for the Browns and was a consistent sack leader. In 1976, he recorded 12 sacks, including a Browns' record of four in a game. In his career, Sherk had 864 tackles and 69 ½ sacks.

# JOHNY HENDRICKS
## ADA & EDMOND

**75**

Known for his powerful punches, Hendricks was born in Ada and was a three-time Oklahoma high school wrestling champion at Edmond Memorial High School. At OSU, he won the national championship title at 165 pounds in 2005 and 2006 and finished second in 2007.

After college, Hendricks signed with Team Takedown and has become a mixed martial artist and fights in the Ultimate Fighting Championship (UFC) Welterweight Division. In 2014, he was UFC Welterweight Champion.

Born in Wewoka and a graduate of East Central University in Ada, Morgan became one of the PGA Senior Tour's most consistent performers. After earning a Doctor of Optometry degree in 1972, Morgan turned professional as a golfer. He won seven events on the PGA Tour from 1977 to 1990. His most prestigious win on the PGA tour was the 1978 World Series of Golf. He played on Ryder Cup

teams in 1979 and 1983.

In the 1992 U.S. Open at Pebble Beach, California, Morgan was the first player in the championship's history to reach ten under par, eventually going to 12 under. He joined the Senior Tour in 1996 and promptly was named Rookie of the Year. He won the Byron Nelson Award as the tour's top player in 2000 and 2001. Three of his 24 wins through 2009 were in Senior Tour major championships, The Tradition, in 1997 and 1998, and the Senior Players Championship in 1998.

Courtesy Oklahoma Sports Hall of Fame.

## ARNOLD SHORT
### WEATHERFORD & OKLAHOMA CITY UNIVERSITY

**77**

Playing for legendary Coach Abe Lemons at OCU, Short, a graduate of Weatherford High School, became OCU's first basketball All American in 1953. He repeated the honor the following year. He still owns several OCU basketball records, including 23 free throws made in a game. It was at that time the NCAA record. Short was a major reason OCU won the All-College tournament in 1953. He was named the MVP after scoring 70 points in three games.

After college, Short was a two-time, first-team All-Star for the Phillips 66ers team in the National Industrial Basketball League. He later was OCU's head tennis coach, assistant basketball coach, athletic director, and was tennis pro at the Oklahoma City Tennis Center. He is an ordained minister in the United Methodist Church.

## DON BUTLER
**TULSA**

# 78

One of the original stars of professional fishing, Butler won the second Bassmasters Classic in 1972. He founded the "Okiebug" tackle business in Tulsa, and was the first member of the Bass Anglers Sportsman Society (BASS). The organization's founder, Ray Scott, credited Butler with helping make BASS the world's largest fishing group. Scott said, "No other human being had a more profound impact on the fulfillment of my vision than Don Butler."

# GLENN DOBBS 79
## FREDERICK & UNIVERSITY OF TULSA

Dobbs graduated from Frederick High School as a star tailback and punter. He was a single-wing halfback on University of Tulsa teams that had a combined record of 25-6. He led the Golden Hurricane to national football prominence with Sun Bowl and Sugar Bowl appearances in 1942 and 1943.

A member of the College Football Hall of Fame, Dobbs was a first-team All American selection in his final college season in which he led the nation in pass completion percentage. He was called college football's first "quad back," able to pass, punt, run with the ball, or defend against the opposition. He still holds several TU football records.

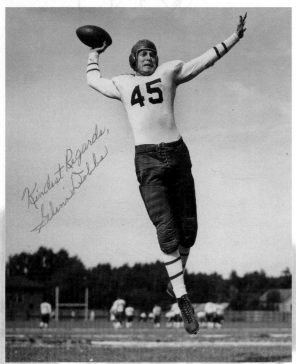

Dobbs played nine seasons in professional football with the Brooklyn Dodgers, Los Angeles Dons, Saskatchewan Roughriders, and Hamilton Tiger-Cats.

He was head football coach at TU from 1961 to 1968, posting a 45-37 record. His teams led the nation in passing three times. He was also TU's athletic director. He died in 2002.

# LINDY MCDANIEL
## HOLLIS & UNIVERSITY OF OKLAHOMA

**80**

Lindy McDaniel

PITCHER    ST. LOUIS CARDINALS

*Courtesy The Topps Company Inc.*

Born in Hollis, McDaniel pitched one season for OU before skipping the minor leagues to go straight to the majors. Pitching mostly in relief, he played 21 major league seasons and retired with 987 appearances, second only to Hoyt Wilhelm.

A right-handed, control pitcher, McDaniel was quietly consistent in the bullpen for the Cardinals, Cubs, Giants, Yankees, and Royals. He was selected to the National League All Star team in 1960. He led the league in saves in 1959, 1960, and 1963. *The Sporting News* named him the Reliever of the Year in the National League in 1960 and 1963.

As a Yankee in 1970, he had a career-high 29 saves, tying a franchise record. He played in 225 consecutive games in the National League without committing an error—a record. He once retired 32 straight hitters in August, 1968. He is among major league baseball's career leaders in saves. A deeply religious man, McDaniel became a Church of Christ minister after retiring from baseball in 1975.

A native of Dallas, Texas, Verplank played golf at OSU. While a Cowboy, he won the Western Open, the first amateur to win a PGA tour event in 30 years. He also won the 1984 U.S. Amateur Championship at Edmond's Oak Tree Golf Club and was the NCAA individual title winner in the national championship tournament.

After graduating from OSU, Verplank turned pro in 1986. He has five PGA tour wins and made Ryder Cup appearances in 2002 and 2006. With diabetes, he received the 2002 Ben Hogan Award, given by the Golf Writers Association of American to a player who has  continued to be active in golf despite a physical handicap or serious illness. He was also named the PGA Tour Comeback Player of the Year in 1998.

In 2006, Verplank became the first American player to ever sink a hole-in-one in Ryder Cup play.

# BRYANT REEVES

## GANS & OKLAHOMA STATE UNIVERSITY

## 82

"Big Country" went to high school in Gans, Oklahoma, and got his nickname from OSU basketball teammate Byron Houston after Reeves was amazed at his first airplane flight across the country. At seven feet tall and 275 pounds, Reeves was an imposing physical presence on the basketball court. He averaged 21.5 points per game as a senior at OSU and led the Cowboys to the 1995 Final Four.

Reeves was the sixth overall pick in the 1995 NBA draft, selected by the Vancouver Grizzlies. He played six seasons in the NBA for the Grizzlies. In 1997, he averaged 16.2 points per game and was awarded a six-year, $61.8 million contract. His best season was 1997-1998, averaging 16.3 points, 7.9 rebounds, and 1.08 blocked shots per game. Reeves retired from the NBA midway through the 2001-2002 season.

# BOBBY USSERY
## VIAN
# 83

A member of the American Thoroughbred Horse Racing Hall of Fame and the National Museum of Racing Hall of Fame, Ussery was born in Vian. He began his career as a jockey in 1951 at age 16 and by the end of the decade had won several major races and Canada's most prestigious race, the Queen's Plate.

In 1960 Ussery won several races riding Bally Ache, including a second-place finish in the Kentucky Derby and a win in the Preakness Stakes. In 1967, he won the Kentucky Derby on Proud Clarion and was victorious again the following year on Dancer's Image.

Ussery retired in 1974 with 3,611 victories as one of the nation's most successful jockeys in the middle decades of the twentieth century.

# SAM BRADFORD 84
## OKLAHOMA CITY & UNIVERSITY OF OKLAHOMA

Bradford was born in Oklahoma City and starred in football, basketball, and golf at Putnam City North High School. At OU, he became only the second sophomore to win the Heisman Trophy in 2008. He holds the NCAA record for most touchdown passes by a freshman quarterback.

Bradford was selected by the St. Louis Rams as the top overall pick in the 2010 NFL draft. In his first season, he was the NFL Offensive Rookie of the Year and set the league record for most completions by a rookie and for most consecutive passes without an interception by a rookie.

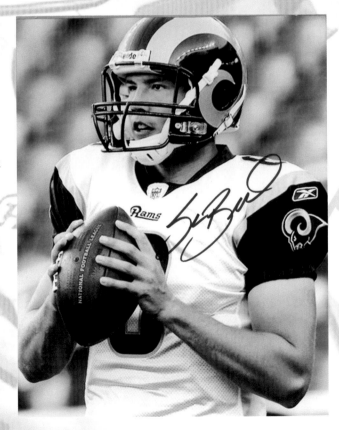

# DREW PEARSON
## UNIVERSITY OF TULSA

In high school in New Jersey, Pearson succeeded Joe Theismann as quarterback. As a flanker for a run-oriented University of Tulsa team, he caught 33 passes and won the President's Award for being the "best spirited and most unselfish" member of the team.

The Dallas Cowboys signed Pearson as a free agent in 1973. In 11 seasons for Dallas, Pearson became respected as one of the NFL's greatest wide receivers, with 489 career receptions for 7,822 yards. He was named to the NFL 1970s All-Decade Team and was selected as one of the Top 20 Pro Football All-Time Wide Receivers.

Pearson was selected for the Pro Bowl three times. He led the National Football Conference in pass receptions in 1976 and was Cowboys' offensive captain in four seasons. He played in three Super Bowls and scored a touchdown in Super Bowl X. One of his memorable moments was catching the "Hail Mary" from Roger Staubach in a 1975 playoff game. In 2009, the NFL Network listed him tenth on the list of the greatest Dallas Cowboys.

# KELLY GARRISON
## ALTUS & UNIVERSITY OF OKLAHOMA

Garrison, a native of Altus, barely missed making the United States Olympic gymnastics team at age 12 in 1980. Four years later, she was named an alternate, but did not get to compete in the Olympics.

A star gymnast at OU, Garrison won back-to-back NCAA All-Around championships in 1987 and 1988. She finished second in the United States Olympic trials in 1988 and wound up 16th in the All-Around competition at the Summer Olympic Games in Seoul, Korea, and was seventh on the balance beam. From age 11, Garrison had the same coach, Becky Buwick, who also coached her at OU.

After suffering a series of nagging injuries, Garrison retired from gymnastics at age 21 in 1988.

*Courtesy University of Oklahoma Department of Athletics.*

# JERRY TUBBS
## UNIVERSITY OF OKLAHOMA

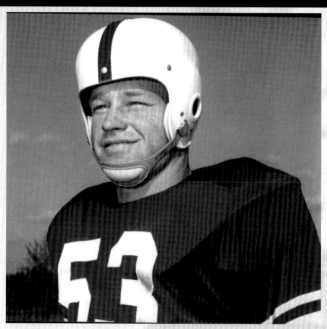

A member of the College Football Hall of Fame, Tubbs was a three-time All State football player in Texas before playing his college career at OU. He was varsity team captain in 1956. He never played a losing game at OU while the Sooners were on their way to the 47-game winning streak. He was part of the national champion teams in 1954 and 1955. He was consensus All American in 1955 and 1956 and was the first Sooner to win the Walter Camp Award as the nation's outstanding football player. He was voted the outstanding lineman in 1956 in every poll and finished fourth in that year's Heisman Trophy vote.

Tubbs was drafted by the Chicago Cardinals in the first round of the 1957 NFL draft. He played linebacker from 1957 to 1966 for the Cardinals, San Francisco 49ers, and Dallas Cowboys. He was All-Pro in 1962 and was the Dallas Cowboys' team captain four years.

When Tubbs retired as a player, he became the linebackers coach under Tom Landry for 21 years. He coached in five Super Bowls, Dallas winning two of them.

# MATT KEMP
## MIDWEST CITY

**88**

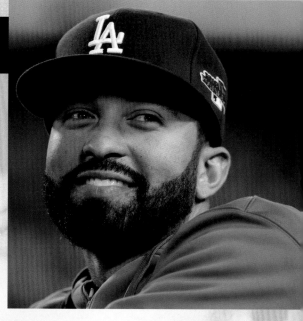

Kemp was born in Midwest City and starred in basketball and baseball at Midwest City High School. His basketball team won back-to-back state titles. After high school, he was drafted by the Los Angeles Dodgers in the sixth round of the 2003 major league baseball draft. After three seasons in the minors, he made his debut with the Dodgers in 2006. He became a starting outfielder in 2008.

Kemp is a two-time All-Star and led the National League in home runs, runs batted in, and runs scored in 2011. He was second in the Most Valuable Player balloting to Ryan Braun. Kemp was *Baseball America's* Major League Player of the Year, was the first Dodger to win the Hank Aaron Award as the top hitter in the National League, and signed a franchise record $160-million contract. He was traded to the San Diego Padres after the 2014 season.

## BILLY CASKEY
### TULSA ROUGHNECKS

# 89

Tulsa soccer fans still yell "Bring back Billy Caskey!," a reference to the play of the legendary midfielder from Northern Ireland. Shortly after beginning his career in professional soccer, Caskey played on loan to the Tulsa Roughnecks of the North American Soccer League (NASL) from the Glentoran team in Northern Ireland. He played with the Roughnecks until 1985 when he moved to the Dallas Sidekicks.

As a Roughneck, Caskey scored 22 goals in 128 games, although a broken leg sidelined him in 1983 when Tulsa won the NASL championship. He was known for being among the league leaders in penalty minutes. He was later expelled from the Major Indoor Soccer League for assaulting a referee.

Caskey was a member of the Northern Ireland national football team from 1978 to 1982.

## JOHN STARKS
### TULSA & OKLAHOMA STATE UNIVERSITY

**90**

Born in Tulsa and a graduate of Central High School, Starks played basketball for several community colleges before completing his collegiate career at OSU. He was passed over in the NBA draft and played his way into the NBA with stops in the Continental Basketball Association and the World Basketball League.

He played 15 seasons in the NBA with the Golden State Warriors, New York Knicks, Chicago Bulls, and Utah Jazz, retiring in 2002. He was named to the NBA All Star team in 1994 and won the NBA Sixth Man of the Year Award in 1997. After retiring as a player, Starks was hired as a television analyst by the Knicks and worked in the Knicks front office.

Casillas was born in Tulsa and was an All-State football player for East Central High School. He was a consensus first-team All American at OU in 1984 and 1985 and won the Lombardi Award in 1985 as the nation's top lineman. A member of the College Football Hall of Fame, he helped the Sooners win the 1985 national championship. The National Football Foundation named him the College Defensive Player of the Decade for the 1980s.

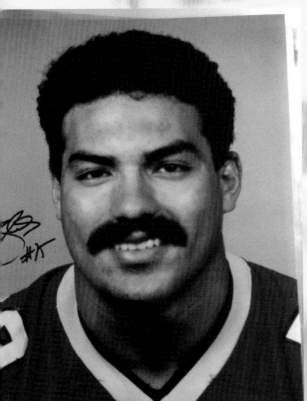

Casillas was the second overall pick in the 1986 NFL draft, selected by the Atlanta Falcons. He played 13 seasons in the NFL as a dominating defensive tackle for the Falcons, Dallas Cowboys, and New York Jets. He was twice named All-Pro and helped the Cowboys win back-to-back Super Bowls XXVII and XXVIII.

# JEFF BENNETT
## VINITA & OKLAHOMA CHRISTIAN COLLEGE

# 92

At 5'8" and 152 pounds, Bennett was known as the "little big man" in the decathlon competition at the 1972 Olympic Games in Munich, Germany. Bennett, a native of Vinita and track and field star at Oklahoma Christian College, was on active duty in the United States Army when he competed for a spot on the Olympic decathlon team in the summer of 1972.

Already the national AAU champion in the decathlon, ten grueling events over two days, Bennett won the pole-vaulting and 400-meter dash competitions in the Olympic trials to win a trip to Munich. Despite competing in a world of giants who were vying to be called the "greatest athlete in the world," Bennett held his own and finished fourth in the Olympic decathlon. He was first among the 33 decathlon competitors in pole vault and placed second in the 400 and 1,500 meters. The four-time NAIA All American, Bennett still holds Oklahoma Christian records in hurdles and decathlon. He is a member of the NAIA Hall of Fame.

After the Olympics, Bennett continued to compete in AAU events. In 1976, he set the American amateur record in pole vault. He tied the record in finishing among the leaders in the AAU decathlon the following year. He most recently was on the athletic staff at Oklahoma Christian University.

## TOM CHURCHILL
**OKLAHOMA CITY & UNIVERSITY OF OKLAHOMA**

**93**

One of the state's greatest all-around athletes, Churchill earned ten letters in four sports at OU, played professional baseball, and competed in the decathlon at the Olympic Games. Born in Blair, Oklahoma, he attended Central High School in Oklahoma City and lettered in football, basketball, baseball, track, and swimming. He was selected by *The Daily Oklahoman* as the best all-around athlete in the state in 1925.

At OU, Churchill was all-conference in basketball, a champion boxer, an All American in football, and winner of the decathlon at the 1928 Kansas Relays. He earned a spot on the United States Olympic team and finished fifth in a field of 38 of the world's greatest athletes at the Olympic Games in 1928 in Amsterdam.

After college, Churchill signed a professional baseball contract with the New York Yankees before an injured shoulder ended his career.

# WES WELKER
## OKLAHOMA CITY

**94**

Ray Soldan says Welker was the best high school football player he ever saw in covering high school sports in Oklahoma for more than 50 years. Born in Oklahoma City, Welker starred for Heritage Hall High School on both offense and defense and as a kicker, winning the state championship his junior year. In 1999, he was named *The Daily Oklahoman* All-State Player of the Year.

Welker was not highly recruited because of his size, but accepted a scholarship at Texas Tech University. He earned the nickname "The Natural" and established himself as a big-game performer as a Red Raider. In four years at Tech, he had 259 receptions for 3,019 yards and 21 touchdowns. He also rushed for another 456 yards. His eight career punt-return touchdowns is an NCAA record.

Undrafted in the 2004 NFL draft, Welker signed as a free agent with the San Diego Chargers. After two years with the Miami Dolphins, Welker came into his own at New England in 2007 when he tied for the NFL lead with 112 receptions. He holds the two highest single season reception totals in New England history and is tied for the NFL record for longest touchdown pass (99 yards). In 2013, he was traded to the Denver Broncos. He is a five-time Pro-Bowler and has led the NFL in receiving yards three times.

In her prime, Yan Fang was the best softball second baseman in the world. Born in Beijing, China, she played college softball at Oklahoma City University. She still holds the OCU softball record for career average, .463.

Yan Fang was an NAIA first-team All American for three seasons from 1997 to 1999. She made the All-Tournament team at the NAIA Championships in 1997 and 1998. She was NAIA Player of the Year in 1998 and 1999.

Yan Fang helped her home country win the silver medal in women's softball at the 1996 Olympic Games.

# JERRY SHIPP 96
## BLUE & SOUTHEASTERN OKLAHOMA STATE

Born in Louisiana, Shipp ended up in home for orphans in Tipton, Oklahoma, at age two. He was adopted by Ed and Ozella Shipp of Blue, a tiny town east of Durant, Oklahoma. A three-year starter on the Blue High School basketball team, Shipp attended college only a few miles from home, playing for Coach Bloomer Sullivan at Southeastern Oklahoma State College. An NAIA All American, Shipp led his 1957 team to the national championship game.

After college, Shipp played five seasons with the Phillips 66ers in Bartlesville. He became the 66ers' fourth-leading scorer of all-time and a three-time AAU All American. With one of the quickest jump shots in basketball, Shipp played in more than 40 games in international competition. He was the leading scorer of the American team in the 1963 Pan American Games, the 1963 World Games, and the 1964 Olympic Games. He was the veteran of the American international competition teams that included Bill Bradley, Willis Reed, and Walt Hazzard.

An Oklahoma City native and football star at Southeast High School, McCoy was recruited by several major NCAA schools but chose to play college football at nearby OU. A consensus All-

American at OU in 2008 and 2009, he was a finalist for the Lombardi Award in 2009. He was a Sooner co-captain two years and started all 40 games during his career.

McCoy was drafted by the Tampa Bay Buccaneers with the third overall pick of the 2010 NFL draft. He is a three-time Pro-Bowler and was First Team All-Pro in 2013. *Pro Football Focus* ranked him as the NFL's Best Defensive Tackle for 2013.

# ROBIN VENTURA
## OKLAHOMA STATE UNIVERSITY

**98**

After attending high school in his native California, Ventura was a three-time All American in baseball at OSU. After leading the nation in runs, runs batted in, and total bases in 1986, he had an NCAA Division I record 58-game hitting streak in 1987. He helped OSU reach the finals of the 1987 College World Series and was a member of the gold medal-winning Olympic baseball team in 1988.

A member of the National College Baseball Hall of Fame, he played 16 years in the major leagues for four teams, the Chicago White Sox, New York Mets, New York Yankees, and Los Angeles Dodgers. He was an All Star in 1992 and 2002 and won the Gold Glove Award at third base six times. Ventura spent most of his career with the White Sox. In 1991, he set a team record for runs batted in at third base and led the American League in putouts. In 1995, he became the eighth player in major league history to hit two grand slams in one game, the first since Frank Robinson 25 years before. The following year, he set White Sox records for homers and grand slams by a third baseman. He retired from baseball in 2004. In 2012 he became manager of the White Sox.

# SERGE IBAKA
## OKLAHOMA CITY THUNDER
# 99

Ibaka was born in the Republic of the Congo, the third-youngest of 18 children. Both his father and mother were basketball players. Ibaka's father was taken prisoner during internal strife in the Congo, so the future NBA star moved to France at age 17, then to Spain, where he became a member of the Spanish National Team.

Ibaka was selected by the Seattle SuperSonics as the 24th pick in the 2008 NBA draft. Six days later, the franchise moved to Oklahoma City. After development in Europe, Ibaka joined the Thunder in 2009. His shot-blocking talent gave him the nicknames of "Air Congo," "Serge Protector," and "Iblocka." He led the NBA in blocks-per-game in 2012 and 2013, and in total number of blocks in four of the past five seasons. He has been named to the NBA All-Defensive First Team three times. His outreach to the Oklahoma community has won Ibaka many devoted fans.

# 100

## VIRGIL FRANKLIN
### RIVERSIDE INDIAN SCHOOL

Franklin was the first Native American to win a national Golden Gloves boxing championship. In 1945, he was a student at the Riverside Indian School in his hometown of Anadarko, Oklahoma. Riverside is the nation's oldest federally operated American Indian boarding school.

Franklin began boxing at age 12 and thundered his way to the 1945 Golden Gloves featherweight title at 126 pounds before more than 20,000 screaming fans at the Chicago Stadium. National boxing writers called him "the greatest puncher in the nation for his size." Franklin won the national crown despite a spill from the ring "when he missed a wallop and landed on a press table outside the ropes." A newspaper reporter observed, "His opponent was still around when the last round was over, but he looked like he might have been in a collision with a fire truck."

# HONORABLE MENTION

In developing any list, there is a valid argument for including athletes not chosen by our method. The following athletes certainly deserve consideration because their performances made them legends and an integral part of Oklahoma sports history. Included in this Honorable Mention list are Oklahoma athletes who had outstanding collegiate careers but did not choose to compete at the professional level or, because of injury or other circumstances, did not have outstanding careers at the highest level of competition for their sport. For example, two of the University of Oklahoma's Heisman Trophy winners did not make our Top 100 list because of lack of success at the professional level. Not making the Top 100 list takes nothing away from their incredible careers and acquiring thousands of admiring fans.

In 1962, **FRECKLES BROWN** became the oldest man to ever win the rodeo title of World Champion Bullrider. He was the first cowboy to ride the legendary bull known as Tornado.

A member of the College Football Hall of Fame, **BOB FENIMORE** was known as the "Blonde Bomber." Born in Woodward, he was Oklahoma A & M's first two-time All-American and led the nation in total offense in 1944 and 1945.

**MATT HOLLIDAY** of Stillwater was number 35 on *The Sporting News* 2009 list of the top 50 players in major league baseball. He has played for the Colorado Rockies and St. Louis Cardinals.

*Courtesy Southwestern Oklahoma State University.*

**KELLI LITSCH** led the Southwestern Oklahoma State University women's basketball team to three national championships. A four-time All American, she was the first woman basketball player inducted into the NAIA Hall of Fame. She no doubt is one of the greatest women college basketball stars of all time. She ended her college career with a record of 129-5 and as the NAIA all-time record holder in points scored with 2,700. She still holds the Oklahoma state high school tournament career scoring record of 37.6 points per game. At Thomas High School, she won two six-on-six state titles and her 3,364 points were at the time the most ever points scored by any player, boy or girl, in Oklahoma high school history. After college, Litsch joined her alma mater as an assistant coach and served many years as assistant athletic director.

**J.W. MASHBURN** of Oklahoma City's Capitol Hill High School was a four-time All American track star at Oklahoma A & M and won a gold medal in the 1952 Olympic Games and at the Pan American Games in 1955. He was honored as Oklahoma's greatest quartermiler.

**COURTNEY PARIS** of OU, a four-time All American, was named the nation's top women's basketball player in 2007 and 2008.

**JERRY RHOME** played his final two college seasons at the University of Tulsa and made shambles of NCAA passing records. He was second in the 1964 Heisman Trophy race and played six years in the NFL.

**BOB TWAY** was an outstanding golfer at OSU and was the PGA Player of the Year in 1986 after posting four tour wins including the PGA Championship.

**HOWARD TWILLEY** shattered school and national records as a receiver at the University of Tulsa. He won the NCAA scoring crown twice. He was the first player in NCAA history to win both the scoring and pass receiving titles in a single season. He was runnerup for the Heisman Trophy in 1965. He played 11 seasons for the Miami Dolphins of the NFL.

OU's first Heisman Trophy winner, **BILLY VESSELS** was born in Cleveland, Oklahoma, where the football stadium is named for him. He led the OU Sooners to the national championship in 1950, and is a member of the College Football Hall of Fame.

At OU, **WAYNE WELLS** was the Sooners' winningest wrestler of all time with a record of 69-4-2. He was a two-time All American at OU, was runner-up in the 1967 NCAA championships at 152 pounds, and won the NCAA crown at that weight in 1968. Wells completed law school and passed the Oklahoma bar examination in 1972 just weeks before competing in the Olympic Games in Munich. He dominated the Olympic competition, winning all seven matches and taking the gold medal.

Raised in Tuttle, **JASON WHITE** was an excellent passing quarterback at OU. After suffering reconstructive surgeries to both knees in the 2001 and 2002 seasons, White made one of sports' greatest comebacks in 2003 to win the Heisman Trophy, the Davey O'Brien Award, and several other national awards. He was a consensus All American and received a medical hardship from the NCAA and was allowed to play a second senior year in 2004. His bad knees prevented him from moving to the NFL.

A Tulsa native, **JACK ZINK** is a legend in the world of car racing as a driver, team leader, mechanic, and engineer. In a 1957 Pontiac he built and designed for the early NASCAR circuit, he set a flying mile speed record. His victories at the famed Indianapolis Motor Speedway and the Indianapolis 500 have earned him a place in racing history. Twice, his team won the coveted Borg Warner Trophy, in back-to-back Indy victories in 1955 and 1956.

The Fellowship of Christian Athletes (FCA), one of the world's most successful ministries to athletes, began in Oklahoma in 1954. Don McClanen, head basketball coach at Eastern Oklahoma State College in Wilburton, wanted to use star Christian athletes to present their testimonies to athletes at the junior high, high school, college, and professional levels.

To promote his idea, McClanen sent a letter to 19 famous athletes and sports figures. Most of them responded and the national FCA movement began as a shoestring operation in Norman, Oklahoma. For the past 60 years Oklahoma FCA leaders have played a prominent role in the worldwide success of FCA.

# THE BIRTH OF THE OKLAHOMA SPORTS HALL OF FAME

Good ideas are usually the result of a lifetime of experiences. But when they finally surface in your brain, they are likely to strike in an instant. So it was, late one evening in 1984, when I was driving home from my television job and heard on radio that Olympic marathoner Joan Benoit had been inducted into the Maine Sports Hall of Fame. Maine? Maine had a sports hall of fame? And Oklahoma didn't? Well, why don't I try and start one.

The list of sports heroes from Oklahoma is truly incredible and it was hard for me to imagine that we weren't doing more to honor our athletes and coaches for all they had done for our state. The next day, I got on the telephone and called Steve Owens (who I knew) and Allie Reynolds (who I didn't) to gauge interest. Soon, I contacted Glen Dobbs in Tulsa to see what interest there might be up there. They all thought it was a good idea and eventually agreed to serve as an early, honorary board. Of course, today, all three are inductees.

About a month later, I set up an appointment with Lee Allan Smith who was the general manager at Oklahoma City's channel four and had a reputation for organizing successful projects. I needed advice. At age 26, walking in to visit the boss of a competing station, I was both scared and intimidated. Lee Allan could not have been more supportive. He also warned me that starting an organization from scratch, in a difficult economy, would not be easy and would take a lot of work.

My advantage was that I didn't know what I didn't know and plunged ahead. The next significant step was getting Jerry McConnell, sports editor of *The Daily Oklahoman*, to recognize the idea as legitimate.

We started producing a series of star-heavy, but low-key, induction banquets. Three years later, I met Lynne Draper who turned the idea to the high-end event it is today.

Now, looking at the list of inductees, and the list of those likely to be inducted in the future, having an Oklahoma Sports Hall of Fame seems like a natural hit. But, in reality, it's been a slow and steady marathon. If Joan Benoit only knew.

MICK CORNETT
Mayor of Oklahoma City

# MEMBERS OF THE OKLAHOMA SPORTS HALL OF FAME

1956 Frederick High School
Alvan Adams
Troy Aikman
Neill Armstrong
Hubert "Geese" Ausbie
Bob Barry, Sr.
Robert E. "Bob" Bass
Wayne Baughman
Johnny Bench
Clayton I. Bennett
Susie Maxwell Berning
Jim Bolding
Harry "The Cat" Brecheen
Freckles Brown
Rick Bryan
Joe Carter
Tony Casillas
Tom Catlin
Don Chandler
Tom Churchill
Charles Coe
Nadia Comaneci
Bart Conner
Bill Connors, Jr.
Roy Dale Cooper

Mick Cornett

Eddie Crowder

Bob Dellinger

Don Demeter

Bob Dickson

Glen Dobbs

Bruce Drake

Lynne Draper

Stanley Draper, Jr.

Tommy Evans

Bob Fenimore

U. C. Ferguson

Eddie Fisher

Ed Gallagher

Walt Garrison

Prentice Gautt

Caesar "Zip" Gayles

Elvan George

Curt Gowdy

Art Griffith

LeRoy "Ace" Gutowsky

Paul Hansen

James Bedford Harris

Labron Harris

Don Haskins

Marques Haynes
Danny Hodge
Mike Holder
Carl Hubbell
Henry P. "Hank" Iba
Pete Incaviglia
Keith Jackson
Jack "Indian Jack" Jacobs
John Jacobs
Ferguson Jenkins
Pat Jones
Harold Keith
Jon Kolb
Bob Kurland
Steve Largent
Abe Lemons
Kelli Litsch
E. M. "Jim" Lookabaugh
Mickey Mantle
J. D. Martin
John Leonard Roosevelt "Pepper" Martin
J. W. Mashburn
Perry Maxwell
Lyndall "Lindy" McDaniel
Tommy McDonald
Cal McLish
Dale McNamara

Don McNeill

Clem McSpadden

Volney Meece

Jack Mildren

Shannon Miller

L. Dale Mitchell

Kenny Monday

Orville Moody

Gil Morgan

Bobby Murcer

Sean O'Grady

Oklahoma Presbyterian College

Leslie O'Neal

Bennie Owen

Steve Owen

Steve Owens

Ted Owens

Andy Payne

Drew Pearson

T. Boone Pickens

Darrell Ray Porter

Mark Price

Greg Pruitt

Jesse "Cab" Rennick

Allie Reynolds

Jerry Rhome

J. D. Roberts

Porter G. "Port" Robertson
Crystal Robinson
Myron Roderick
Wilber "Bullet Joe" Rogan
Darrell Royal
Barry Sanders
Bill Self, Jr.
Dewey Selmon
Lee Roy Selmon
Lucious Selmon
Jerry Shipp
Arnold Short
Jim Shoulders
Jenks Simmons
Billy Sims
John Smith
Michele Smith
Dick Soergel
Ray Soldan
Warren Spahn
John Starks
Bloomer Sullivan
Eddie Sutton
Barry Switzer
Bertha Teague
Bill Teegins

Doug Tewell
Clendon Thomas
Thurman Thomas
Jim Thorpe
Wayman Tisdale
Billy Tubbs
Jerry Tubbs
Gerald Tucker
Bob Tway
Howard Twilley
Jack VanBebber
Billy Vessels
Lloyd Waner
Paul Waner
Gary Ward
John Henry Ward
Joe Washington
J. C. Watts
Jim Weatherall
Wayne Wells
C. B. "Bud" Wilkinson
Paul Young
Walter Young
John S. "Jack" Zink